ORGANIC GARDENING'S

SOIL
FIRST AID
MANUAL

by the editors of ORGANIC GARDENING®
Magazine

CONTENTS

Building the Soil Naturally

You can't put too much organic matter on your garden, but you certainly can overwork yourself.

MARK KANE

When I started gardening, my clay soil was fit for pottery—heavy and sticky in the spring, and hard as adobe in the summer. The first season I spread 45 bales of straw and hay and tilled them in. According to my arithmetic, the clay should have turned into good soil, but by midsummer it turned to brick instead.

After two years I had turned under 80 bales of hay and straw and four wagonloads of manure—enought manure to fill a dump truck—and they had disappeared. The only sign of change was that, walking through the garden, I no longer picked up ten pounds of clay on each boot. Since I never had any trouble getting hay, straw and manure, it took me some time to realize that I was squandering organic matter—and my own labor.

In those first years I spread and tilled in organic matter in spring, and planted by the instructions on the seed packet, laying out rows two and three feet apart. Then I tilled and hoed and weeded until the soil around my plants was as bare as a grade school playground. All that cultivation and bare ground burned up my organic matter. What I gave with one hand, I took away with the other. I put organic matter where no plants grew, and then helped it vanish. Instead, I could have concentrated it on half the ground, grown just as much food, and done more good for the soil.

All this time, there was a good example of natural soil-building right under my garden fence. Falling down from age, the fence was overgrown with weeds, grass and tree sprouts which had raised a ridge of soil and roots three inches higher than the surrounding ground. The bottom wire of the fence was engulfed, and in some places pinned down by roots that took an ax to sever. The soil was light and crumbly, nothing like the heavy clay in my garden and the adjacent pasture.

Where did that ridge of good soil come from? The fencerow plants made it. Plants are the only producers of organic matter, and they know how to use it. They mulch themselves with their own leaves and toppled stems, sheltering the soil from the elements and providing a small, steady supply of organic matter to feed soil life.

On the average, half of all fresh organic matter is transformed to humus in just two months by the bacteria, fungi, insects and animals that teem in the top six inches of soil. Their numbers are as dizzying as a night full of stars—a gram of soil may hold 100 million bacteria, and in an acre of topsoil the bacteria may weigh three tons. There are thousands of species of soil life, each with its specialty. Earthworms, for example, feed on litter, dragging it into their burrows. That's the main reason mulch disappears. I mulch my asparagus patch each fall with six inches of hay, and the old mulch is so thin that when I kneel under the plumes of foliage to spread the hay, I can see the ground and the worm holes.

Mulch is not the only soil-builder. Roots contribute astonishing quantities of organic matter and put it directly in the soil, some of it far deeper than I would care to dig. Roots are also the main agents in making the soil lighter and more open because their probing—and some cement drawn from humus—bonds soil particles together into long-lived aggregates, the "crumbs" the mark of rich soil.

At the end of the second season, I planted winter rye for a cover crop. When I tilled it in near the end of March, the rye was 12 inches high and the roots were so thick they looked like small mops. (One admirable researcher tape-measured a rye plant and found 387 miles of roots and over 6,000 miles of root hairs.) Instead of the cold clods I expected to turn up, the soil shattered into crumbs: Where the garden had gone bare all winter, the soil clung to my boots, but where the rye had grown, I had a seedbed ready for planting.

Between the winter rye and the overgrown fencerow, I finally learned my lesson. A garden can't produce as much organic matter as the same patch of ground would if nature did the gardening. And we gardeners shouldn't expect it to. But we can see to it that our gardens produce as much of their own organic matter as possible and do as much of their own soil-building as possible. That way, the organic matter we supply to make up the deficit will go further.

The main problem with my early soil-building efforts was too much bare ground and not enough plants. I was squeezing nature out of a job and overworking myself, fetching organic matter and turning it in when plants could have done more to build the soil. Humus was burning up. Nutrients were leaching down without roots to catch and bring them up. Aggregates were being destroyed faster than plants could build them.

We should adopt methods that conserve organic matter and humus instead of burning them up. Here are the rules I've learned to follow:

Keep the soil planted. Bare soil should make you shudder. Wherever the soil is neither mulched nor growing plants, you can be sure organic matter is being consumed and nothing is replacing it. Plan for mature plants being close enough to shade the ground. Where you're not growing food, grow a cover crop. Remember that you can't build soil without plants.

Plant in wide rows or beds. Both let you cover more ground with plants than narrow rows, and concentrate organic matter where the plants will grow. With beds 3½ feet wide and paths 18 inches wide, less than 30 percent of your garden goes bare, while with narrow rows and wide paths, as much as two-thirds of your garden is bare (and you do all that cultivating or haul enough mulch to cover it all).

Cultivate sparingly. Cultivation exposes the soil to drying, which breaks apart aggregates and releases the humus that cements them. At the next rain, the plants get a boost from the released humus, but beware of gardeners who boast that this is a benefit of cultivation.

You pay for the benefit with your soil's organic matter.

Cultivation also speeds up the oxidation of organic matter and humus, burning up your supply faster than plants can capture and use it.

From what I have read, there's nothing to the idea that cultivation during dry spells makes a "dust mulch" that keeps water in the soil. Once the soil surface has dried out, there's no difference in the rate of evaporation whether the soil is cultivated, undisturbed or mulched. Of course, the mulched soil holds water longer.

Keep the soil mulched. Soil life needs constant feeding. It's better to put organic matter or compost in the soil in small, regular amounts than to turn under your whole supply at the beginning of the season. If you give the soil one big feeding, you'll get a microbial population explosion and then a collapse. Nothing feeds the soil better, with less work from the gardener, than mulch.

When I put my garden in wide beds, I didn't want even the paths to go bare, so I dug them out to a depth of eight inches, spreading the soil on the beds, and filling them with sawdust. Watching the sawdust drop year by year—it's down about three inches in four years—gives me the smug feeling that nature's making topsoil out of the clay underneath. .

Put your organic matter in the topsoil. There's no point in burying organic matter deeply. Nature keeps humus in the top six inches of soil and so should you. That's where the soil life is.

About 85 percent of all roots are in the first six inches of soil. The ones that go deeper are mainly in search of water. They leave a modest amount of organic matter in the subsoil, but it turns to humus only slowly, since there is very little oxygen to support soil life. Most of the subsoil nutrients leach down from the topsoil or are released by acids.

Once I began to cooperate with nature, my soil improved quickly. I saw the usual signs: lots of earthworms, dark, crumbly soil replacing clay, and so on. But the most dramatic sign was the appearance of new and thriving weeds, like dock, with its long lancelike leaves and yellow root, that never gives up sprouting no matter how many times it's cut. Dock annoys me, but it makes me proud, too.

A final point about organic matter: There's a limit to how much your soil can use efficiently, and it's not set by how many pickup loads of manure you can haul in a season. In the North, where cool summers slow down the loss of humus, you can pat yourself on the back if you build up the organic matter in your soil to 4 percent. In the South, where hot, humid summers burn up humus, you'll have to work hard to reach 2 percent. Of course, you can put on as much organic matter as you like, or have energy for, and you *can* surpass the natural limits. I don't go out of my way to try, however. I'd rather be gardening.

A Program to Build Fertile Soil

*How do you get from ordinary dirt
to ever-richer organic soil?
Let us count the ways.*

GENE LOGSDON

Here's what we're shooting for in a good, organic garden soil—deep, crumbly, water-absorbent, nutrient-rich loam filled with actively-decaying organic matter and bursting with the microscopic life that shows itself in *results*.

To get a garden full of this kind of superior growing medium, it takes about three years of high-powered fertilization, followed by yearly applications of enough organic matter to keep plant nutrients high.

Some folks start with a soil test—and they can be interesting if you want to know about your soil's chemistry. But if you are interested primarily in the size of your cabbage and the lusciousness of your tomatoes, such testing isn't necessary. The right soil fertility program will bring your garden to a peak of nutrition and mellow the soil to the proper pH—automatically.

And that's because expert organic gardeners with small-scale plots depend on three elements that do all these things for them: manure, compost and mulch. There are variations and frills that help—such as a barrel of manure tea—but, manure, compost and mulch are the keys.

Let's look at these individually.

Manure. Applications of fresh manure must rot down in the soil before planting. Till it in as early as possible in the spring—at least three weeks before planting. Or add it in the fall, and follow up with compost in the spring if you want to plant as soon as the soil thaws out.

Compost. Here's the keystone of the organic method. It's hard to make enough to fertilize the entire garden, so make as much as you can and use it as a ready-to-use, all-purpose fertilizer throughout the growing season. Concentrate it right where the plants are growing for best effect. It won't burn plants, and it contains the rock powders through which you are adding nutrients like potash, phosphorus and trace elements.

Mulch. Mulches add your actively decaying organic matter, which is necessary to produce the organic acids in the soil that unlock your garden's real yield potential. Try for mulches that are essentially nutritious, such as clover or alfalfa.

We recommend the following soil fertility program for the average backyard garden. Embellish as you see fit.

First Three Years

1. Till in heavy applications of manure in early spring.
2. Concentrate as much compost as possible under and around your plants. You can apply it anytime.
3. Use good, thick mulches starting as soon as the soil warms

up—usually around the end of May or early June.

4. Either till under a fall application of manure or sow a green manure crop like clover, to be turned under in the spring.

In the first three years, manure applications should be four inches thick, or two inches if you use extra-rich chicken manure. Compost everything you can and use as much as you make, since you are trying to get your soil to be as close to compost as possible. Mulches are generally from 6 to 12 inches thick, depending on the plants' sizes, enough to keep down weeds.

Every Year Thereafter

After three years of the foregoing treatment—plus your extras (leaves, buried kitchen garbage, seaweed or whatever you find during the year)—your soil will be cooking. Now the trick is to keep it cooking. That's done with yearly additions of plant matter used as mulch and with compost. Keep your soil covered with rotted leaves spoiled hay, rotted bark or other mulches. They will decay from the bottom, enriching the soil continually through the year. Continue to make as much compost as possible, and use it liberally during the peak growing months when plants are putting on growth and demand the most from the soil.

The above is only a general guideline. Now let's look at some actual practices. Gene Hiers' garden, in Charlotte, North Carolina, for instance, is kept cooking with just leaves.

Gene tills under two 12-inch layers of shredded leaves in the fall, along with a sprinkling of lime. Then in summer he mulches his growing vegetables with a third 12-inch layer of leaves. That's his fertility program. All of it. Works too, as the bounty of his 1,600 square feet of garden shows. "Except for a few whiteflies on fall greens, no bugs last year either," he says. University of North Carolina soil tests reveal his garden has ample amounts of all necessary nutrients, while his organic matter content has steadily increased to nearly 5 percent.

Glenn Robertson, in Nashville, Tennessee, follows a more meticulous program in his French intensive matrix garden. For tomato plants, for example, he prepares holes 22 inches in diameter and 24 inches deep, which he fills with 40 gallons of his own fertilizer mixture: "Two cups of bone meal, 10 gallons of rotted horse manure—not cow manure—10 gallons of compost, and 20 gallons of a mixture of 9 gallons of topsoil screened through ½-inch hardware cloth, 4½ gallons of coarse builder's sand, and 6½ gallons of shredded leaves. Do this in the fall preceding planting so that the earthworms have time to turn much of the bed's ingredients into castings, which are one of the richest fertilizers known," says Robertson. In soil beds like this, with the treatment repeated every year, Robertson raises tomatoes that produce 75 to 100 pounds of fruit per plant and far more total vegetables than his family can consume in only about 800 square feet of garden space.

My own gardening endeavors cover about 2½ acres of vegetables, fruit trees, kitchen grains, permanent rows of asparagus, grapes and raspberries, and four beds of strawberries rotated with peas, fall greens and melons. So I have had to develop, by trial and error, a fertility program that would allow me to get all the work done and keep yields up. Here's how I do it in my various gardens.

The No-Till Mulch Garden

Here we raise annual vegetables that do not take much room. This plot has never been plowed. Each fall I pile leaves beside it and spread them on the garden the next year when the vegetables are up and growing well. I put a layer of manure on top of the leaves in June, about four to six inches deep, along with a sprinkling of wood ashes from the stove. The ash application amounts to about a cupful per plant. All garden residues are shredded with the rotary mower and left on the garden, even the seeds. I spread the pomace from cider-making onto the garden in the fall, too. Few weeds grow, but very many volunteer vegetables and little apple trees come up each spring, which is all right with me. Eventually, we may not have to plant at all but just thin the volunteer stand! (I pull the volunteers now, or transplant someplace else.)

Time involved? Since the manure has to be hauled and the leaves must be raked off the lawn anyway, the time used in mulching this garden is minimal.

Permanent Vegetables—Asparagus, Rhubarb, Onions

The annual accumulation of chicken manure goes on these crops in June after we quit cutting the asparagus. Almost all our kitchen scraps have been composted into this manure too—by the chickens. Everyone has to work on this homestead, and chickens are the best composters as they scratch in their bedding. Again, little time is involved because the chicken coop has to be cleaned out, asparagus or no asparagus.

The Strawberry Beds and Raspberry Rows

Fertilizing these parts of my garden is a bit complicated, and will be clearer if you look at the following drawing.

Rows	Beds
A—Grapes	1—First-year strawberries
B—Asparagus	2—Second-year strawberries
C thru I—Raspberries	3—Third-year strawberries
	plus melons (interplanted)
	4—Fourth-year peas—fall greens

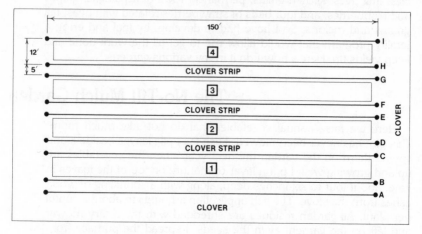

The rows are permanent and the beds are rotated—4 to 1 to 2 to 3 and back to 4 again. Each bed has its fertilizer application depending on which part of the rotation it's currently in. In the drawing, bed #1 we'll assume two new berries have just been planted (in April here). As soon as time permits in May, I apply a heavy coating of rotted cow manure over the entire bed, snuggling it up as close to the new plants as possible to block weed growth, and also layering manure on the permanent rows (B and C) on either side of the bed. In the following winter, I spread a thin layer of straw over the entire bed, plants and all. This should be straw never rained on, as rain will leach potash out of straw in a hurry.

In bed #2, the straw mulch of the previous winter is raked in April to the edges of the bed, making ready for the harvest. The straw raked to the edges serves at the same time to mulch the rows of raspberries (D and E) on either side. After strawberry harvest, the plants are mowed off, the clippings allowed to lay on the surface for mulch. At this time (July), I place a light layer of manure along the edges and between the strawberry rows, for the new runners to grow onto. The manure on the outside edges fertilizes the raspberries in rows D and E, too.

In bed #3, the last year for the berries, I interplant melons down the middle in May, unceremoniously pulling out berry plants that might block the sun to the melons. The berry harvest is completed just as the melons begin to vine. The berry plants are then rotary-

14

tilled into the soil, but no other fertilizer is applied. The melons grow wonderfully on the decaying mulch and manure of previous years. The raspberry canes on either side of the bed are given a late fall mulch of leaves, but I don't spread them into the beds.

In bed #4, peas are planted early in rows and the bed is kept clean-cultivated, including the raspberries on either side, the leaves along the raspberries being tilled in at the same time the rest of the bed is prepared for peas. This year-long clean cultivation is good for the raspberries, which in a continuous mulch-gardening situation begin to develop grassy weed problems in 3 to 4 years. The peas are fertilized with a mixture of one part blood meal (or what we call meat scraps or tankage) and one part wood ashes, in a band along the row, about a pint's worth per foot of row. A similar application I dribble along the raspberries on either side of the bed.

The narrower strips of ground between the pairs of raspberry rows (C–D, E–F, G–H) are planted to white clover, as indicated, and these strips I mow regularly, the clippings falling around the base of the canes for additional mulch. The clover strips are mostly for looks though—and to encourage the bees.

Time involved in fertilizing the beds is the equivalent of two solid weekends, the way I work, though it could be done faster. Most of the time is involved in the hauling.

The Orchard

Fertilizing the orchard is easiest of all. The first couple of years I spread a 6- to 8-inch layer of manure around each tree out to the drip line in the winter, followed by an equal layer of fresh-cut clover in summer. I was getting too much vegetative growth on the trees from the manure, so now I limit fertilization to the summer clover mulch. If it rots away by winter, I may add leaves every other year. I now pile fall mulch near the trees (or I pull it back from around them) to let the ground freeze around the trees and to discourage mice. Then I put the mulch in place in early spring before the ground thaws. The longer I can keep the ground frozen, the longer I can keep the trees from breaking dormancy, and so less chance of blossom kill from late frosts. I practice this on strawberries, too.

Garden Grains and Annual Vegetables that Require Much Space

These foods are grown on a field plot in rotation with other plots of alfalfa and grains for livestock. The grains include corn for meal, sweet corn, popcorn, sorghum for syrup, plus onions, potatoes and beans of various kinds. Basically, the fertilizer program for these crops is green manure. In the rotation, these crops follow three years of alfalfa, at least one cutting of which is shredded back onto the soil as mulch, and the last cutting of which is plowed under for green manure when knee-high. In a moist fall, an alfalfa planting where a cutting or two has been allowed to rot back into the soil is extremely rich in earthworms. Wheat and other small grains, sweet potatoes and beans following such alfalfa receive no other fertilizer at all and do very well. The Irish potatoes I mulch with manure in addition— but they still do not grow well for me, the only food that so far I've had only mediocre results with in this kind of program.

The onions receive a side-dressing of blood meal and wood ashes as described for the peas. Over the newly planted corn and sorghum seed, I apply a 4-inch band, one to two inches thick, of the following mixture: 10 parts crumbly, composted manure, one part blood meal, and one part wood ashes. I guess rather than mix exactly. What I actually do is throw about 20 forkfuls of the manure on the truck, then about 35 pounds each of ashes and meal, then 20 more fork-fuls of manure and so on until the truck bed is about ¾ full. It takes two loads this size to cover the rows. As I shovel it out on the corn, the layers of manure, meal and ashes mix together adequately enough for my purpose.

The application over the corn and sorghum rows does more than just fertilize. It acts as a protective shield to the soil, which is clayish and will crust badly if a hard rain falls on it after planting. Corn, particularly sweet corn, and especially the better white varieties, have a very difficult time coming up through a crusted soil surface. The manure, meal and ash mixture prevents crusting over the row. This also explains why the manure mixture must be a crumbly, composted consistency. The little corn shoots would not be able to pry their way up through chunks of manure either.

At the same time, the band of manure over the row seems to discourage (but does not altogether prevent) birds from pecking down into the ground and eating the sprouted corn kernels. The mulch also slows weed growth around the emerging corn shoots, and being a dark color, absorbs and transfers warmth from the sun to the soil around the sprouts at that critical germinating time when plants need all the warmth they can get. Finally, the mulch-banding marks the rows so that I can cultivate between them with a tiller even before the corn comes up.

I treat about 20 rows of corn in this manner, each about 150 feet long. The job is not easy and takes half a day to complete, but there is a certain satisfaction I derive from its effectiveness which makes it pleasant for me.

At the end of the growing season, this plot of kitchen grains and vegetables receives a coating of manure at the rate of about 10 tons per acre (two pickup loads per quarter acre), and the ground is then plowed.

You quickly see that the basic difference between my soil maintenance methods and those of both Hiers and Robertson is that my methods are built on *surface* mulching of organic materials, while theirs are based on tilling or mixing the organic materials down deep *into* the soil. My opinion is that their method is better, or at least effective more quickly, since in essence they do in one year what it takes me three or four to accomplish. But the fertilizing process is the same in both cases. Robertson composts his organic material first, then mixes it in the soil. I spread my organic materials on the soil, allow them to sheet-compost as mulch over a period of years, and *then* till or plow them into the soil. My method works better for me in a big garden, since I also control weeds, temperature and moisture while saving the time of building and managing the large compost heaps that would be necessary for me. Summing up: Robertson's and Hiers' methods fit the small gardener better. Mine mesh well with the activities of a larger homestead. But all three methods and variations on them will keep soil rich.

How do I *know* my soil is getting richer every year? Every year the plants are healthier and yield more. Every year the soil increases in tilth and water absorption. If I had a problem, I would take a soil sample. But I've concluded that soil analysis has only limited value except where soil is being stressed with heavy application of concentrated fertilizers and chemicals toxic to soil life or capable of making some soil nutrients unavailable to plants, as some herbicides seem to do. Even then, commercial farmers tell me that soil sampling can only tell what is in the soil, not how much is *available* to the plant. Some growers do leaf-analysis testing, but that will tell you only what's in the plant, not what is left in the soil. Using both tests, commercial growers feel they have a better indication of their fertility conditions, but they also point out that two testing labs may make different recommendations and analyses of the same samples. And they tell me that the same soil will test higher in some nutrients in summer than in winter.

I used to play around with the soil-testing kits people like to give gardeners for Christmas. I enjoyed doing that and I think the kits have some value in making new gardeners more aware of what they are doing. But I never could determine with any precision what my soil needed from these.

Gardening in Sandy Soil

*Some simple steps can build
your sandy soil into fertile,
crop-producing loam.*

MICHAEL GOC

Where I live in Wisconsin, the soil is so sandy that we still have several moving dunes—a strange miniature Sahara on the edge of the northwoods. Nevertheless, I've been able to grow delicious vegetables after practicing some easy methods of soil improvement.

The most important improvement to sandy soil is the addition of lots of organic matter. You can hardly overdo it. Manure and compost or other rotted plant material such as leaves should be worked into the soil, followed by a mulch of leaves, grass clippings, wood chips, bark, hay or straw. These mulches absorb water and hide it away from the sun. The soil beneath stays cooler, and its organic matter hangs onto moisture that has slipped through the mulch. Sandy soil drains so fast that a lot of rain can disappear before plant roots get any of it. But water that trickles slowly through mulch takes more time getting into the soil and to the roots. Instead of a quick flood, most of which is wasted, the plants receive a smaller, steadier trickle which can be used. The gardener who mulches his rows uses his own form of drip irrigation without all the fancy equipment.

Sandy soil can be mulched at any time, but the first mulch of spring is best applied right after a rain. Since sand drains so well, there is little danger of mold forming.

A rotary-tiller will run through mulched sand like a paddle-wheel steamer churns downstream. The mulch is mixed into the sand quickly, decomposing rapidly into a rich humus, which will improve the soil's texture and its water—and nutrient-holding capacity.

Although sandy soil needs organic improvement, it does have some advantages over lumpy clay. Sandy soil is easier to work—you don't need a size 13 workboot stomping on your shovel to turn it over. Compaction is never a problem—what is a garden path one year may be easily planted the next. And the fine grains of sand mix easily into compost. Mulch can be quickly worked or tilled into sandy soil. In fact, all the mixing and stirring required by most tillage systems is simpler in sand.

Sandy soil's good drainage is both an asset and a liability. Less moisture is likely to remain locked into sand when it freezes in early winter. That means it can be worked earlier in the spring—a plus for Northern gardeners. Likewise, an excessively wet spring will not delay planting very long. Puddles rarely last long on top of sand. It sucks up moisture in one big slurp. Add normal evaporation to fast drainage, and you have near-drought conditions.

Water, then, is the chief concern of the sandy-soil gardener. But there is more to managing water than just turning on the sprinkler and forgetting about it—a habit that is both wasteful and unnecessary.

Planting drought-resistant varieties is one easy way to utilize available moisture. Some of the vegetables I have found that do well in sandy soil are the WANDO pea, CHERRY BELLE radish, RUBY QUEEN

The right "Companions" can keep your garden cool all summer long!

beet, MARGLOBE and RUTGERS tomatoes, CHALLENGER cucumber, CHANTENAY carrot and MAMMOTH RUSSIAN sunflowers.

Companion planting is another way to step up productivity in sandy soil. You can plant with several advantages in mind—insect control, efficient use of space, and compatibility. You can also interplant to produce shady areas. Root plants love sand, cool weather and water. Help them out by surrounding your cool-weather-loving plants with tall standing ones to give them shade. Bushy tomato plants are good shade givers, along with sunflowers and sweet corn. All three get higher as the season gets hotter, providing more shade just when the roots need it most.

I use roots for animal feed, so they make up an extensive part of my garden. Carrots, mangels, sugar beets, turnips, kohlrabi and red beets are left in the ground from April planting until November harvest. The entire root patch will be bounded, even crossed, with rows of tomatoes or sweet corn. Every fourth or fifth row of roots is interrupted by a single parallel row of sunflowers. The summer sun travels high in the sky so shade plants must be plentiful and close to the roots they are protecting.

We've found that MAMMOTH RUSSIAN sunflowers, with their wrist-thick stalks and table-napkin-size leaves, make the most shade. Each plant is a cylinder of regularly shaped leaves that forms a tower of shade reaching across rows of roots just when they need it. And the delicious sunflower seeds are an extra bonus.

Another planting method that helps hold moisture in sandy soil utilizes those ground-hugging travelers, the squash vines. Squash planted in hills at the ends of the root rows can be trained to grow right down the aisle between them. Most gardeners have their root crops thinned long before the squash vines get big enough to trip them up. And, quite obligingly, squash vines die off with the first frost, before the roots are harvested. It's easy to use the canopy provided by the vines to protect and cool the soil next to the roots, prevent evaporation, and shade out late-sprouting weeds.

Some plants, such as onions and potatoes, prefer cool temperatures but need lots of sunshine. A row of low bushy plants, like green beans, planted between every two rows of onions, shades the soil, but not too much to hurt the bulbs.

Potatoes grow best with mulch. Sandy soil covered with hay or straw mulch is potato heaven. All the plants in your garden will benefit from mulching, as will your soil.

Gardening in sandy soil can be a challenge for any green thumb, but there are steps you can take to make the task easier and your garden more productive.

Simple Ways to Soften Your Soil

Hard soil can break your back, your spirit, and maybe even your bank account. Follow these practical, easy-to-do techniques, and you can save all three.

ANTHONY DeCROSTA

Some time ago I decided to rent a small house and start my first garden. The landlord, who lived next door, offered to let me use a piece of land behind his place, where a previous tenant had grown some vegetables. After borrowing a shovel, I went out to look over the plot and plan my gardening strategy. Immediately I realized that it was going to be much more difficult than I first thought.

Caramel-colored, the soil seemed as barren as an asteroid. Rocks—some the size of footballs—jutted through the surface. Others lay buried wherever the point of the shovel probed. It was as unlikely a garden plot as I could imagine, and looking beyond the property line I quickly understood why. A track of duplex houses was being built nearby, and the topsoil in the area had been pummeled by bulldozers and dump trucks.

The next evening I returned with a pickax and began digging up the rocks. I worked for a week—sometimes in the rain when the crusty soil turned to thick syrup under my feet—before I cleared a 400-square-foot area. Maybe my garden wouldn't be a big one, I reasoned, but at least it would supply me with a few essential crops. After turning over the soil with a rented rotary tiller, I raked the small stones and clods of dirt to the side, and planted my seeds.

Nothing grew, of course. Perhaps that doesn't surprise you. But it not only surprised me, it ruined by appetite for gardening for a long time. I didn't try working a piece of land again until I had moved away from that house.

I tell this story for a good reason. Once soil has been severely damaged, it takes time to recover. Many gardeners solve the problem of hard soil by incorporating organic matter—in the form of compost, mulches and green manures—into their gardens. After one year the soil loosens somewhat, after two it gets crumbly, and after three it is rich and friable. *But what about this year?* What's the best strategy to turn hard soil soft so that you can do some gardening before the season runs out?

In an attempt to answer this question, I talked to a number of soil experts and home gardeners. The advice they give can be summarized in three points:

* Work on a small scale at first, using enriched soil in planting holes or furrows.

* If a soil is dominated by one texture, incorporate its opposite (e.g., sand with clays).

* Introduce organic matter into your garden as the key to both short- and long-term soil enrichment.

What Makes Soil Hard?

Soil is constantly being created by the same chemical, physical and biological elements which formed it originally eons ago—decaying plant matter, climate, glacial forces and the action of tiny organisms like bacteria, fungi, actinomycetes and yeasts on the rocks of the earth. Soil formation is a slow process—scientists say it takes over 500 years to make an inch of soil—but deep down at bedrock, subsoil is always being made. When humus or other organic matter is added, either naturally or through conscientious gardening practices, loams or topsoils are produced.

The difference between hard soil and soft soil is a *textural* one. Soil experts use the term texture to express the relative proportion of different-sized particles in a particular soil. Parent rocks containing quartz, feldspar, hornblende and calcite—plus other basic minerals—weather into sands, silts and clays. Sand particles, the largest and most irregular of the three, measure from 1/50 to 1/500 inch. Silt particles range from 1/500 to 1/2,500 inch, and clay particles are less than 1/12,500 of an inch—so minute they cannot be seen with an ordinary microscope. Almost every soil has some percentage of sand, silt and clay in it. Just how much of each determines what kind of soil problem you're going to have to tackle. The ability of the soil to absorb nutrients and water, along with its porosity and tilth, all depend on the particle size.

Because sand particles are so coarse, and because the spaces between them are comparatively large, they do not tend to stick together or granulate. Even when wet, such particles cannot be molded. Water passes rapidly through them—which is obvious to anybody living in the Southwest when a thunderstorm strikes. The water disappears as quickly as it comes. Soils dominated by sand possess good drainage and aeration, and are usually in a loose, open condition. Unfortunately, they expose so little surface compared to an equal weight of silt or clay particles that the part they play in the chemical and physical activities of the soil is small. In other words, sand particles are *inactive*. "Their chief function in soil is to serve as a framework around which the active part of the soil is associated," note three Michigan State University soil scientists in their book, *Fundamentals of Soil Science*.

At the other end of the texture scale, clay is composed of particles so fine it binds up easily when wet. Clay may have thousands of times more surface area per gram than silt and nearly a million times more surface area than very coarse sand. These numbers are significant for a gardener. Because the amount of surface area in clay is much greater than that in an equal weight of sand or silt, its water-holding capacity—as well as its ability to hold essential nutrients—is much greater, too. Clay (along with humus) acts as a storage reservoir for both water and nutrients. Unlike sand, clay particles are very reactive, constantly taking on and giving up ions of other elements in the soil. But soils dominated by clay (40 to 60 percent) become sticky and practically unmanageable when wet, and hard and cloddy

24

CHARACTERISTICS OF SOIL SEPARATES

Separate	Diameter mm*	Number of Particles per Gram	Surface Area in 1 Gram, sq cm
Very coarse sand	2.00-1.00	90	11
Coarse sand	1.00-0.50	720	23
Medium sand	0.50-0.25	5,700	45
Fine sand	0.25-0.10	46,000	91
Very fine sand	0.10-0.05	722,000	227
Silt	0.05-0.002	5,776,000	454
Clay	Below 0.002	90,260,853,000	8,000,000

*United States Department of Agriculture System.

This chart shows how the size of soil particles affects soil texture. A gram of clay contains many more particles and much more surface area than an equal weight of sand.

when dry. They're called heavy soils for good reason—they're very tough to work with. The pore spaces are too small for air, plant roots or soil water to penetrate readily. Poor aeration causes a decrease in the activity of soil microorganisms, which are so prevalent in good loam soil, which has 40 to 60 percent of its bulk occupied with pore space.

You don't need expensive lab equipment to determine the texture of your soil. Looking at it isn't enough, though—soils tend to take on the color of their parent material, which can be any number of different hues. Instead, perform this simple test:

Place some soil in the palm of your hand and wet it slightly. (Spit works well.) Then gently rub the mixture with two fingers. Sand feels gritty. Silt feels like moist talcum powder. Clay is hard when dry, slippery when wet, and rubbery when moist. If you can roll the sample into a thin snake between your palms without it falling apart, your soil has a very high clay content, and you and your crops will probably suffer because of it.

Of course, having too much clay is not the only factor that can make your soil tough. Pressure from your own footsteps or the frequent passage of heavy machinery over garden beds will form hardpans—impenetrable layers of compacted soil a few inches below the surfaces that impede root growth and water penetration. Also, topsoil can be eroded by wind or rain, leaving hard subsoil exposed. It takes nature hundreds of years to restore such a soil's tilth and fertility. With organic methods, the natural process can be speeded up, and we can be planting even in the worst soils in one year.

How to Soften Soil

Dick Harwood knows soils. For most of his life he has worked the land—every kind of land from gravelly sands to subsoil clays. And as Director of the Organic Gardening and Farming Research Center, he has talked to many gardeners hard put to find a solution for hard soil. One common error, he says, is that they try to do too much too fast.

"If you have to work in a miserable, heavy soil, take a small area and do a good job with that," he explains. "The main principle is to get lots of organic matter—compost, mulch, well-rotted manure—into the soil—*deep* into the soil. As the organic matter decomposes, the growth of bacteria, fungi and microorganisms is encouraged. The whole biological activity of the soil is enhanced. Remember that you're dealing with a complex biological system. Work to improve the overall health of the land."

According to Dr. Harwood, the best way to get organic matter deep into the soil where it can do the most good is to use either the French Intensive method of double-digging, or the trench or posthole methods. These techniques will break up the soil without breaking your back. And the organic matter you layer in will feed hungry microbes, which will have an added softening effect while conserving water.

Some gardeners blend in sand or gravel to physically lighten their unmanageable land. But these will work only if the soil is heavy clay. Again, the object for the first year is to start on a small scale. "Take an area about as big as a room and work in a 10 to 20 percent mixture of sand or gravel," Dr. Harwood says.

Some other tips to soften—or avoid—hard soils:

*Don't turn over your garden in the fall and leave it exposed to the weather. Rains will compact the soil and the cold weather will destroy beneficial microorganisms. Instead, spread mulch or litter for protection. Turn the mulch over just before spring planting.

*Tilling helps only when the soil has the right moisture content. If it's too wet, clods will form. If it's too dry, the soil will just crumble to dust. "At the farm, we like to leave the soil a little cloddy," Dr. Harwood says. "That way we don't have so much of a weed problem."

*If you try subsoiling to correct hardpan, don't mix the subsoil in with the topsoil. "You don't want to upset the natural soil horizons and levels," he cautions. "Subsoiling is very difficult for the home gardener to do, anyway. Double-digging works a lot better."

*When you water your crops, use a fine spray rather than a steady, heavy stream. This will prevent "puddling," which damages upper-level soil structure.

*While green manures incorporate organic matter into the soil, a gardener usually has to correct any nutritional problems first, or the crop will not grow. A drawback to using green manures initially on a tough soil is that the garden must be taken out of production while the clover or alfalfa grows. But green manures have a part in maintaining fertile soils.

*Salt—either the halite type used for ice on sidewalks in the winter, or the kind used in water softeners—destroys the aggregation of soil particles. Keep salt off your table and out of your garden!

"You should consider your soil as a long-term investment," says Dr. Harwood. "If you treat it right, you'll cash in on that investment for many years."

Rich Compost in Three Weeks

---

*You don't need a lot of space
and you don't need to wait to get
compost working in your garden.*

JACK RUTTLE

Fast compost—unlike fast food—is the very best kind you can make. There are only two tricks to producing it. When you put the pile together, you have to create just the right balance of carbon to nitrogen that a fast-working heap likes. Once you know a little about the materials you are working with, that's quite easy to do. I use grass clippings and leaves, but there are many other good combinations. You also have to keep the pile supplied with plenty of air, which takes some hard work.

Rapid decomposition burns up oxygen fast. A well-made pile will heat up in two days. But to keep it rotting as quickly as it is able requires a turning for aeration every second or third day. Without it, the bacteria and fungi that are digesting the pile run out of oxygen and the decomposition slows. Turning means that matted clumps have to be hacked and torn apart, not just flipped from one spot to another. Turning a 3-by-3-by-8-foot pile takes me about 45 minutes the first three or four times. After the compost is half rotted, the turning becomes much easier.

Why bother with all that work? I could just as effectively build a big compost pile and let it rot by itself for half a year. Well yes, that can work too, but in my particular situation that method can't sustain my garden. One batch of compost a year isn't enough.

My yard is only 20 feet wide. I have 90 feet to garden in between the back door and the alley. There is no room for a truck or trailer to haul in compostables, and not much room for a compost pile—if we're to plant much garden. We take a lot of food from that little patch of land. We start picking from a 15-by-5-foot cold frame in March and finish out the season from the frame about January 1. There are five other beds the same size as the cold frame and a modest flower and herb garden. There are 30 feet of raspberries and two strawberry beds that require an inch of compost mulch each season. Most of the time there's a little more food coming from the garden than two people can eat. Fast compost keeps all that going.

Fast composting gives me *three* batches of compost from my 5-by-15-foot compost bin each season. If I needed more, and I had the materials and energy to make the heaps, I could certainly double the production. But I'm happy as it is.

There's another reason for learning to make a pile that will compost fast—no matter what turning schedule you use. It's a foolproof test of how well you are proportioning materials. If the mix is right, the pile will heat up within 24 hours after a turning. If the mix is poor in nitrogen (or too rich in carbohydrates—another way of saying the same thing), nothing else you might try will make it heat. You'll know by instinct how to blend all sorts of materials together correctly after three or four successful fast compost piles. The experience will put an end to piles that rot only partially after a *year* of sitting. An end to piles that smell funny when you open them for spreading on the garden.

To start building a pile, all you need to know is a rough estimate of the carbon and nitrogen content of the materials you have to work with. The carbon content is a gauge of the food energy (everything from simple sugars in fruits and vegetable wastes to complex, hard-to-digest carbohydrates like stem fibers and wood) that is available for the microbes. The microbes also use nitrogen as building blocks for protein as they multiply. They must have both these things to fire a population explosion big enough to devour an entire compost heap.

To work at peak efficiency, the bacteria and fungi in a compost pile need 25 to 30 parts of carbon to one part nitrogen. If there is too much carbon, the microbial expansion will use up all the nitrogen and then stop, leaving extra carbon-bearing material unrotted. The compost won't reach the high-heating stage. Further decomposition creeps along until more nitrogen is available. If you put the half-finished compost on the garden, the microbes will quickly absorb the available *soil* nitrogen, thus robbing your vegetable plants of it.

If there is too much nitrogen—that is, less than 25 parts of carbon to one part nitrogen—the excess will be wasted. You will smell it escaping as ammonia gas when you turn the pile.

When the balance is right (carbon level between 25 and 30), heat-loving microbes thrive. The temperature rises, which makes the microbes work even faster. As a bonus to you, the high heat also kills many weed seeds and disease-causing organisms. Nearly all the nitrogen is incorporated into the bodies of the microorganisms. And they consume carbon energy in the process until the carbon level drops to roughly 10 parts to each part of nitrogen. That's the same carbon-to-nitrogen ratio as a humus-rich soil. The compost then cools to about 110 degrees F. and is ready to go on the garden immediately.

Very few materials contain the perfect balance of these nutrients for fast composting. Good-quality hays and soybean stover do. Fluff them into a pile, moisten them, and they'll rot quite nicely. Most materials you can get easily for composting have to be mixed with something else that will complement their deficiency in carbon or nitrogen. Use the accompanying chart as a gauge when you're getting together the ingredients for a compost pile.

After using the chart for a while, I've learned to judge the carbon and nitrogen content of things by how they look. All fresh green plant matter is higher in nitrogen. So are seed meals like coffee grounds or soybean meal. The older and tougher, brittle parts of plants are higher in carbon. Another sign of high carbon and low nitrogen is a pale or brownish color. More complex carbohydrates like bark, wood and the toughest fibers break down slowly, even with ample nitrogen. Go light on these things in your mixes. Most wastes from animals—manure, urine, blood meal, hair and the like—are high in nitrogen. Fats are high in carbon but are so hard to mix that you are better off not using them.

Grass clippings and leaves are the backbone of my composting system. Both are easy to get. If I lived in the country, I would probably mix manure with spoiled hay, straw or other crop wastes. But all around me tidy townfolk bag up enormous quantities of grass clippings and leaves, then set them on the curb with the trash. Chances are good that if manure and crop residues are rare items in your neighborhood, you can get all the leaves and grass clippings you can carry within distance or a very short drive.

Every fall I fill the empty compost bin with leaves. I pile more bags two deep over the carrot bed, which keeps the carrots fresh and diggable through February. In spring I gather in enough trash bags of fresh grass clippings to use up all the leaves in one big batch of compost. I want to get the land free of the leaves and planted as soon as possible. And I get usable compost in mid-June.

I start the pile with a layer of leaves because they are more absorbent. The materials go on in alternating layers (each three or four inches thick) because it's a convenient way to keep track of proportions while building. The layers disappear completely during the first turning two days later. The proportions of grass to leaves is very roughly one to one by volume. When the pile is three to four feet high, it's finished. I thatch the top with some empty plastic bags held in place with boards or branches. The plastic holds in the water vapor to keep the pile moist and to prevent rain from waterlogging the pile and leaching out nutrients.

Into the side of the finished pile I stick a dial-type soil thermometer with an eight-inch stem. The thermometer doesn't lie. It tells me exactly how well I've made the mix. A good mix will reach 110 to 120 within three days. If it doesn't get hot enough, the pile needs more protein (nitrogen). So I add more grass clippings at the first turning. After the first turning, the temperature should pass the 140-degree mark.

The thermometer also tells *when* to turn the pile. As soon as the temperature begins to drop a little, the pile has run out of oxygen and needs another turning, every second or third day. The compost pile will maintain temperatures between 140 and 160 for the next two to four weeks, depending on how promptly and thoroughly you aerate the heap. You know the compost is nearly finished when it won't heat up no matter how much you turn it. When it drops to 110, it's ready to go onto the garden or to be bagged in plastic for future use as naturally pasteurized potting soil.

The time from start to finish can vary depending on the digestibility of the materials you have used, how well you proportion them and the aeration. Dr. Clarence Golueke, who has devoted much of his life to studying the details of composting, reports total digestion of a small heap made of sycamore leaves, kitchen garbage and old plants from the garden in 12 days. My batches are finished in two to three weeks.

I chop everything and turn the pile with two tools, a mattock and a pitchfork. I start at one end of the pile with the mattock, swinging it like an ax. It slices off a two- or three-inch bite down through all the layers. This breaks up clumps of leaves and mixes everything thoroughly. After I've chopped enough to cramp my working space, I switch to the pitchfork and throw what I've cut into a new pile. Tossing the stuff with the fork adds even more air. Eventually, the whole pile has been moved from one side of the composting area into a new pile at the other side.

The mattock (or grub-hoe) is indispensable for making fast compost with hand tools. It has a very heavy blade that's four-to-six inches wide. If the blade's kept sharp, the weight of it coming down does nearly all the work of cutting. I first learned of this method of composting from a man named Victor Dalpadado, who developed the system as a small and simple industry for people in Colombo, Sri Lanka. He recommended the mattock. I didn't have one and tried to make do with shovels and a spading fork for chopping and mixing the pile. I even broke a hoe handle at it. The next year I got a mattock and what had been grueling work became comfortable and satisfying. The mattock chops everything but woody branches into little pieces that make for easy turning. By crushing stems and tearing things open, the mattock makes entry ways for the microorganisms. Once inside, their digestive juices do the work of further softening and breaking things down.

No matter what you are using to make compost, everything takes on a nice dark brown and earthy color within a week. The outer six-to-eight inches of the pile will become covered with a gray dust— the bodies of actively growing fungi. Fungi prefer to work in the outer layer where it's cooler. Be sure to turn those materials into the center both to let them reach a high heat and to give the fungi fresh material to work on.

The smell of the pile can tell you a lot. Fast compost never smells rotten or putrid. If you've added too much nitrogenous material, the excess will be released as ammonia gas in the first couple of turnings. It will smell strong and may remind you of fresh manure. But that stage will quickly pass. The smell will soon become very earthy, somewhat like mushrooms.

If you add a bowl of fresh kitchen scraps to a healthy, fast compost pile, you won't find anything but eggshells two days later at the next turning. They'll have been eaten.

The pile will shrink before your eyes after each turning. For one thing, as the particles become smaller as a result of the chopping and decomposition, they pack more densely. But also, a lot of carbon

32

CARBON/NITROGEN RATIOS
OF VARIOUS ORGANIC MATERIALS

Food wastes (table scraps)	15-1
Sewage sludge: activated	6-1
Sewage sludge: digested	16-1
Wood	700-1
Sawdust	500-1
Paper	170-1
Grass clippings	19-1
Leaves	a range of 80-1 to 40-1
Fruit wastes	35-1
Rotted manure	20-1
Sugar cane residues	50-1
Cornstalks	60-1
Straw	80-1
Alfalfa hay	12-1
Humus	10-1
Alfalfa	13-1
Green sweetclover	16-1
Mature sweetclover	23-1
Legume-grass hay	25-1
Oat straw	80-1

You want to blend materials so that your compost heap has a carbon to nitrogen ratio of 30 to one. Using the carbon values in the chart (the carbon value is always the large number), put together any combination that averages out to 30. Combine the materials by weight, not volume. After you've made a few good compost piles, you'll be able to forget the numbers and make a fast-heating mix by the look and feel of what you have.

dioxide gas and water vapor is released as the microbes break down the carbohydrates in the mix. Compost scientists say that a pile loses roughly half its weight as it composts. And my experience has been that the pile shrinks to half its original size by the time the temperature drops to 110 degrees.

That's really all there is to successful composting. A pile must have moisture for the organisms to work, but I've never had to add water to get enough. The moisture released by the rotting grass or the water in fresh manure has been plenty, especially since the plastic covering on top of the pile holds most of it in. However, in very dry areas, or when dry sources of nitrogen like seed meals or dried manures are used, it may be necessary to add water for the pile to heat up. The mixture should be moist enough to glisten but not so wet that you can squeeze water from it. If a pile gets too wet, it will start to cool down and stink. Correct the problem by turning it more often to dry it.

I've often read that ground limestone should be added to the pile to neutralize highly acidic materials like oak leaves. I used to do this. But in my research I've found several reasons for *not* adding limestone. Scientists have learned that when the nutrient mix is right for rapid digestion (no matter what the initial pH), the workings of the microbes create a very alkaline pH in the pile during the process. When the digestion is complete, the pH drops down to about 6.5 all by itself. That's just where vegetables like it. Limestone added to a compost pile will also cause a chemical reaction that creates ammonia gas, which in turn wastes nitrogen. So I don't add it to my compost pile, but work it into the soil in spring.

I don't remember where I first heard it, but grass clippings and leaves each have had reputations as ingredients for compost. Obviously that's wrong. The only problem I can imagine with leaves is that they can pack into mats that are the devil to break up. That happens when they sit over the winter in large, soggy piles. But leaves are usually bagged in dry weather. Leaving them in the bags keeps them dry and mixable come spring. Grass clippings don't keep well in bags or in big piles because they rot fast into a foul, gooey mass with a texture like peanut butter. I gather clippings when I'm ready to make compost (they're available after any weekend, spring through fall), and I never hold them in bags longer than a week or two.

After the leaves are gone, I'm short on carbon for composting. For batch numbers two and three, I track down some low-grade hay or straw that a farmer needs to get rid of to make room for the new crop. Often it goes for free, but I've paid up to a dollar a bale for it because I value the compost. Then I have to line up a truck for a few hours and haul the stuff. Mixed with grass clippings, old hay or straw composts a little easier than leaves.

I like this system because it gives us beautiful compost and lots of it. I have made many batches of casual compost over the years in a number of ways—sprinkled limestone all through it, added garden soil to each layer, started the heap on a bed of brush for bottom aeration. But I never got the pasteurizing temperatures I knew I should reach, or had enough finished compost to go around. Learning fast composting has taught me what things in the process really matter. I can count on having compost when I need it.

The method I'm using now is obviously a lot more than a way to handle our own garbage, which is half of what I used to think compost is for. But not much of our food ends up in the garbage. Perhaps if we had more trees and mowed more lawns (and cared a lot more about gathering all that stuff up), then our garden could depend on our own waste recycling efforts. It's become obvious to me now, however, that I've got to give back in compost every bit of the bounty we take out of the garden, plus a forkful or two more for good measure. Fast composting has taught me how I can do that and what I need to go out and get—without being haphazard or wasting a lot of my energy.

The Many Moods of Mulch

From keeping down weeds to keeping up soil moisture and yields, it's a good mulch that makes the big difference!

M. C. GOLDMAN

The value of a layer of material placed on the soil surface is pretty well recognized today by gardeners of all shapes, sizes and sections of the country. Most backyard green-thumbers know that mulching cuts weeding or hoeing, that it holds vital moisture effectively, making extra watering necessary far less often. Most are also aware that a natural mulch benefits plants in other ways—helping to maintain an even soil temperature in weather extremes, easing the planting and harvesting steps, and contributing enrichment to the topsoil as it decomposes and adds humus and minerals.

Several questions still hang like a balsam glider on a balmy spring day, though. What materials make the best mulches? When should they be applied? Should a good mulch always be the same depth, or measured to slide-rule accuracy to function right? How much mulch is enough? Are winter mulches advisable? What other advantages—or drawbacks—can I expect if I try mulching?

New Evidence that Mulch Pays

Over the past several years, testing results and reports of new benefits have piled up like a thick mulch. For example, mulching tomato vines with straw cuts down on crop loss from blossom-end rot, according to North Carolina Experiment Station observations. "The disease is caused by the lack of calcium in the plants," explained Extension agent Roger Hyatt. "If moisture is low in the soil, the plant cannot take up the needed calcium." In one tomato grower's comparison test, losses from blossom-end rot during dry weather were greater in the unmulched plot—and he determined to mulch all of his crops in future seasons. Another way mulch combats plant disease is by preventing crust formation on the topsoil. Ground corncobs, for instance, make a light and bulky topping that helps to "fluff up" the soil. Ohio State horticulturist L. C. Chadwick reports a ground cob mulch helps to prevent black spot on roses.

Vegetable seeds also germinate better when you keep the soil from crusting. Univ. of California tests show materials like vermiculite, partly composted manure and vinyl film scoring high for this purpose. A combination of some produced the greatest stand of lettuce seedlings, while materials such as porous redwood sawdust, medium-fine rock and rice hulls composted with sewerage sludge all gave significant anti-crusting results.

Fighting erosion, especially on sloping ground, is another role mulch fills with gusto. At Nebraska, comparisons made by Agricultural Research Service engineers revealed that wood chips, prairie hay, asphalt and wheat straw checked erosion on 6 percent slopes with up to 98 percent effectiveness.

Boosting yields is yet another mulch benefit, certainly one that counts with home gardeners. At the New Mexico Agricultural Experiment Station, for instance, orchard-management studies showed that apple trees given an alfalfa hay mulch produced larger fruit than trees kept either in permanent sod or under chemical-spray weed control. Grapevines mulched with a layer of straw outyielded cultivated vines by 25 percent at the Ohio Station, where raspberries mulched with wheat straw also showed a 10 percent increase over cultivated plants, as well as a boost in berry size. And at the same station, peat moss or sawdust mulches on blueberries brought as much as 80 to 152 percent higher yields than cultivated berries. Montana Experiment Station tests showed that wheat production more than doubled when growers seeded crops in 24-inch-spaced rows and covered the area between them with such materials as pea-sized gravel, flat rocks or tar paper. The gravel mulch, used for centuries by the Chinese, increased soil water storage from 25 to 45 percent.

The value of mulch for summer and fall-grown beans came across dramatically in tests at Auburn University in Alabama. Eight crops of pole beans were compared for average yields. One with no mulch returned 104 bushels per acre. With a newspaper mulch the yield went to 128 bushels. Dry lespedeza straw raised it to 177 bushels, and pine straw upped the return to 182 bushels to the acre. Peanut hulls increased the harvest to 185 bushels. Oat straw out-distanced all the mulches by returning a polebean yield of 239 bushels per acre. Except for the paper, put on in one-sheet thickness, all the mulch materials were applied at a depth of 1½ to 2 inches, starting before the spring planting, then reused for summer and fall crops. A similar comparison at Auburn showed even bigger differences in tomato yields, with peanut hulls jumping returns from 290 no-mulch bushels per acre to 528.

Overcoming regional soil problems is another mulching achievement. Soil specialists at the Texas Station, for instance, have worked out a "mulch recipe" for reclaiming land in the Rio Grande Delta ruined by salt accumulation. The barren clay-loam plots, so saline they produce almost no crops at all, are covered in March with a 5-inch layer of cotton gin trash (dried bolls, stems and leaves). The plots are left idle at least 6 months, then plowed and planted to crops. Within 5 months of applying 30 tons of mulch per acre, researchers found 84 percent of the salts had been leached from the top 30 inches of soil.

A nonorganic mulch making more news this season is aluminum. Univ. of California researchers have increased melon yields 45 percent by keeping green peach aphids from landing. The aphids spread watermelon mosaic disease. Entomologists laid a mulch of aluminum foil and white plastic to confuse the overflying pests. They say the mulch probably causes the aphids to see reflected ultraviolet light instead of the normal blue-green light of plants that would be a signal to land. Earlier tests at the Univ. of Wisconsin showed similar success in thwarting potato aphids with sky-reflecting aluminum, while the foil mulch reduced bean beetle infestation 80 percent in plots at the USDA's Agricultural Research Center in Beltsville, Md.

Best Mulches for Home Gardens

For the home gardener, the most practical and popular mulches are those easily available and cleanly handled. Baled hay, usually "spoiled" for livestock feed, is readily moved, spread by peeling convenient layers or "books" from the bale—a la Ruth Stout. Leaves and leaf mold, grass clippings, pine needles and coffee grounds (both acid) are helpful, common mulching choices. So too are a variety of waste or by-products of food processing: cocoa and buckwheat hulls, shredded cotton burs and gin trash, ground tree bark, shredded sugar cane (bagasse), and the shells from peanuts, oats, rice or cottonseed.

Shoreline dwellers have seaweed and often salt hay available, both rich in minerals and free of weed seeds. Sawdust is offered at planing mills and wood chips frequently by powerline pruning crews. Spent hops, the waste product of breweries, are quite moist, light-colored, more resistant to fire hazard than straw, and have a beery odor that persists a few weeks. Chopped tobacco stems are coarse, and may help discourage some insect pests. (They're not for tomatoes, though, since they may spread mosaic disease.)

Peat moss, although it doesn't contain any nutrients, improves soil tilth, aeration and drainage, ultimately helping plants absorb nutrients from other materials. An old stand-by, it can be spread an inch or more in vegetable gardens and flower beds, used as a half-inch topdressing twice a year on established lawns.

As for sawdust, there is no basis in fact for many of the old accusations tossed at it. Used properly, it's not a "devil" that sours soil or robs plant food. Weathered or unweathered, from hardwood or softwood, sawdust is not toxic in any way. It is organic matter, beneficial as both a mulch and soil conditioner. Used about 3 inches thick, it serves efficiently around fruit trees, shrubs, perennials, evergreens, and in border plantings. Like other carbon-rich materials, sawdust will sometimes turn plants yellow if used alone. The reason is that soil bacteria and fungi temporarily use so much nitrogen to decompose sawdust that little is left for the plants. The yellowing is a hunger sign—and the difficulty can be prevented by adding any of the nitrogen-rich organic fertilizers, such as compost, manure, blood meal, fish wastes and emulsion, cottonseed or soybean meal, bone meal, etc.

How Much Mulch?

How much mulch do you need? For crops that are in the garden over most of the summer, the thickness of the mulch should be enough to prevent weed growth. A thin layer of finely shredded plant materials is more effective than unshredded loose material. For example, a 4- to 5-inch sawdust layer will hold down weeds as well as 8 or more inches of hay, straw or a similar "open" material. So will one or two inches of buckwheat or cocoa bean hulls, or a 2- to 4-inch depth of pine needles. Leaves and cornstalks should be shredded or mixed with a light material like straw to prevent packing into a soggy mass. In a mixture, unshredded leaves can be spread 8 to 12 inches deep for the winter.

Seaweed is another controversial material. Does it work as well as a mulch? Does it conjure up visions of crabs, clams, sea monsters or mermaids lurking under it? Answering in order: yes, seaweed is a practical, effective mulch where it's available. And, no, it's unlikely to be harboring any of the larger sea inhabitants, although trace mineral values are usually higher in the marine plant wastes.

Edwin Gildner, who lives in Pompton Plains, N.J., told us about seaweed's virtues in no uncertain terms: "For gardeners near the shore, seaweed mulch is an excellent weapon. It will do a fine job of squelching weeds while retaining moisture around plants in hot, dry weather. In fall and winter it prolongs the life of late crops such as beets, carrots, and kale. The insulation provided by seaweed mulch has also been a lifesaver for my mimosa trees and other shrubs during recent severe winters. At all times it gradually disintegrates to improve mineral and tilth qualities of the soil. In addition, it doesn't blow away readily, despite gusty New Jersey coastal winds. Leaves, even when ground up, may blow away. They won't when covered with a layer of seaweed.

"When fall approaches I cover the entire garden with a blanket of seaweed. This foils the early attack of spring weeds. Then when I'm ready to plant, I push aside the mulch just enough so that I can dig each furrow. My garden is quite free of insect pests and sometimes I wonder if the seaweed mulch is at least partly responsible. This gift from Neptune is quite available and can be approached by land or sea. Well, actually by land or bay, since the weed I gather, eel grass (*Zostera marina*) thrives in New Jersey's shallow Barnegat Bay waters. It constantly breaks off, particularly after storms, and floats to the surface. Winds and tides deposit it along beaches and marshy shores in strung out piles called 'grass wrack.'

Years ago gathering eel grass was a local industry along Barnegat Bay. It was dried and sold to manufacturers of glassware for use as packing. It also once served as stuffing in *very* economical mattresses. Now no one seems to want it. So I stuff it in my rowboat or pickup truck and bring it to my garden."

Inland, a small homestead pond in Avon, Ohio, has brought the same advantages to Christine Hilston and her family. "Apparently there is enough water migration through our pond so that it does not stagnate," she writes. "However, the hot weather and resultant water-temperature rise during July and August produce an abundant crop of aquatic plant life in the pond. When we were faced with a drought last summer, an idea began to form. Why not use the pond's plant production as a green, moisture-laden mulch?

"So the 'dredging' operation began. With boots on his feet and a rake in his hands, my husband Paul pulled clump after clump of pond-weeds from the water. The majority consisted of tiny floating duckweed and submerged feathery, delicate-appearing *Myriophyllum*. I hauled load after load to the garden and applied it to the rows of vegetables. In addition to bringing moisture and nutrients from the pond to the vegetables they surrounded, our pondweeds shaded the soil from the burning sun and conserved what little moisture fell from the clouds.

"Did our pondweed mulch benefit our garden? Some sweet corn had been mulched and some had not, giving us a comparison. The mulched corn grew taller, the leaves greener, and ears longer, while the unmulched rows produced stunted plants and ears. We don't know for certain, but we feel that credit should go to our aquatic mulch.

"When summer's heat returns and our pond again produces a super-abundance of plant life, we plan to use it again, either alone or in conjunction with other mulching material. After all, who can resist the aroma of the seashore as the pondweeds dry out during the long sweltering summer heat?"

What about specific crops? Such acid-loving plants as strawberries, blueberries, cranberries, raspberries, peanuts, radishes, sweet potatoes, watermelons, azaleas, camellias, mums, rhododendrons, etc., do well with an acid-material mulch—most leaves, pine needles, sawdust, wood shavings, salt hay. According to the Wisconsin Experimental Station, a 1½-to-2-inch layer of salt hay makes the best mulch for strawberries. Pine needles are another excellent topping for this plant, and have been found effective at a 2- to 4-inch depth. Tests at the Ohio Agricultural Experiment Station showed that mulched blueberries yielded more fruit than cultivated plantings, and that sawdust at a rate of 6 to 8 inches gave the most consistent results.

Actually, a mulch program maintained for several years will let you practically forget about acid or alkaline soil problems. Ample organic matter acts as an effective buffer and helps to neutralize extremes of pH in any soil.

Mulch Timing Is Important

Some vegetables, like tomatoes and corn, need a thoroughly warmed soil to encourage ideal growth. A mulch applied too early in the spring, before ground temperatures have had a chance to climb a little in frost-zone areas, may slow up such crops. Once plants are well started, though, and the weather levels off, mulch is definitely in order to conserve needed water, stimulate topsoil microorganisms, and generally condition the soil.

Author-gardener John Krill pinpointed the importance of logical mulch timing for tomatoes in an ORGANIC GARDENING* magazine report. His experiments—and the experiences of others—show that early ripe tomatoes cannot be expected if the spring-thawing ground is cloaked too soon. In summing up his findings, Ohio gardener Krill writes, "I have learned this lesson: That if mulch is applied before the earth is thoroughly warmed, it will delay the ripening of tomatoes. I apply mulch now only when the flowers are profuse, or may even wait until the fruit sets before mulching the plants. Then the mulch seals the heat in instead of sealing it out. . . . For late-ripening tomatoes I mulch my plants heavily when I set them out. For the earliest possible fruit I set out enough to get ripe tomatoes in un-mulched soil until the juicier and better-flavored tomatoes are ripened in the mulched rows. By the wise use of mulch you can prevent tomatoes ripening all at one time."

Lewis Hill, the Vermont nurseryman, adds: "Like many other organic gardeners, we've discovered that mulch, although it's a perfect gardening tool for all crops in moderate climates, acts as an insulator, which is sometimes good and sometimes not so good in cold climates. It is excellent to use on cool-weather crops, certainly, and it is helpful to keep fruit trees from starting growth and blooming too early in areas where late spring frosts may kill the blooms. It's a good tool for delaying strawberry blooms for the same reason. A cool mulch is not so good when placed on warm-weather crops such as grapes, however, where delayed blooming can shorten the time that they have to mature before frost."

Winter Mulch Aids Plant Survival

Perhaps one of the least appreciated roles filled so well by mulch is at harvesttime and over the winter. When harvesting approaches, vegetables which sprawl on the ground, such as cucumbers, squash, strawberries, unstaked tomatoes, etc., often become moldy or even develop rot. Others may be damaged by falling onto uncovered soil. A mulch prevents such injury by keeping the vegetables clean and dry, and by providing a cushioned layer on which they can rest or drop.

Besides this aid, a late-summer mulch helps to prolong the growing season. By buffering the effects of early frosts, it allows more time for second plantings or late crops to mature. At both ends of the summer, mulched soil and plants derive a noticeable benefit in this guard against weather extremes.

As Indian summer wanes and fall makes its mercury-dropping entrance, the usefulness of a mulch follows the season. There's a somewhat different prime purpose in the fall and winter mulch, though, and it's important to keep this in mind. Protection, that is, from sudden temperature changes, from up-and-down thermometer-readings which can harm over-wintering plants.

The mulch now should be applied *after* the first hard frost to prevent alternate thaws and freezes from heaving soil, roots or bulbs. Its purpose once winter sets in is to hold the lower temperature *in* the soil, avoid a rise and subsequent refreezing which shifts the earth and plants, often exposing enough to cause winterkilling. To protect your shrubs, and particularly roses, mound several inches of earth around them early in autumn, then mulch after the first freeze with several more inches of leaves, straw, yard trimmings, etc. Young trees can be protected from rabbit or field mouse damage by wrapping hardware mesh loosely around their base before the circle of mulch is applied.

Of course, the winter carpet of organic matter also helps condition the whole garden area for the next spring.

How do you choose a good mulch? By what is handy and free or inexpensively available. By where you live, the sort of soil you have, and the crops or plants you're growing. Working out an ideal mulch program takes some experimenting, some trials with various materials and depths. It's only common sense to check on the most plentiful free and reasonable sources, to test the effects of different mulches in your climate locale, your own soil type and timing. But the program more than pays—in handsome dividends of better homegrown foods, a finer soil, and happier gardeners.

Wood Ashes and Your Garden

*Collect ashes from this winter's fires
for fertilizer and pest control
this spring.*

WALTER MASSON

Stockpile the wood ashes from your fireplace or stove this winter and use them this spring as fertilizer supplements for your garden. As your ashes accumulate, store them outdoors in a fireproof container with a lid, or one kept under cover, so nutrients won't be leached by rain and melting snow. I use a metal trash can.

Wood ashes contain two of the basic components of a complete fertilizer, potassium carbonate (potash) and phosphorus (as phosphorus pentoxide), plus the trace elements sodium, magnesium, iron, silicon and sulfur. Ashes are also high in calcium carbonate (a form of lime), making them a speedy way to raise the pH factor of soil. These minerals found in ashes were absorbed by the living tree before it was burnt. The highest percentages are in the hardwoods, especially young trees and twigs.

Almost all charts you find that list the three basic elements in wood ashes differ widely. This is due to the type of tree ash analyzed. I've averaged percentages from a half dozen charts, with results as follows:

100 POUNDS OF DRY, FRESH ASH

Lime (Calcium Carbonate)	Phosphorus (Phosphorus Pentoxide)	Potassium (Potash)
20–53%	3–7%	8–20%

(Plus the trace elements copper, zinc, manganese, iron, sodium and boron.)

Lime serves as a soil alkalizer and is helpful to many plants. Don't put ashes near the acid-lovers, such as blueberries, azaleas and rhododendrons, and keep them out of soil in which potatoes are to be raised, to avoid scab.

Phosphorus stimulates seed growth and root development. It hastens maturity, boosts fruit growth and improves a plant's resistance to diseases and winterkill. It also aids in vitamin development.

Potassium (potash) influences initial root and tuber growth and promotes sturdiness.

Most seed and root vegetables will benefit from applications of wood ashes—peas, beets, carrots, cucumbers, radishes, squash, corn, tomatoes, peppers and bulbous root crops, as well as grapes and other fruits. Salt-lovers, such as asparagus, will be helped by the trace element sodium. Before applying ashes, make a soil test to determine which nutrients are needed.

Put the ashes on your soil in the spring. Dig or rotary-till them under. If put on in the fall, nutrients will be leached by rain and melting snow.

Our forefathers leached lye from wood ashes to make soap. Experienced campers today use ashes for scouring pots and pans. Because the lye content is caustic when wet, it can "burn" seeds,

stems and root hairs of young plants, so keep ashes a few inches from stems and gently hoe under. Spread about five to ten pounds of ashes per 100 square feet.

Many organic gardeners spread wood ashes around their root crops to discourage the egg-laying root maggot fly. Vegetables that usually need this protection are radishes, onions, turnips, cabbages and other brassicas. Cover the ashes lightly with soil so they won't blow away.

Should your plants be bothered by slugs, snails or cutworms, encircle them with a three- to four-inch wide trench, a few inches deep, filled with wood ashes. The pests will avoid crawling over them.

An old-fashioned spray to control flea beetles on tomatoes and other plants is a mixture of wood ashes and water. Add an equal amount of powdered lime, dissolved in soapy water, to use for cucumber beetles. Some other uses for wood ashes are:

* Sprinkle a few cupfuls of ashes, in place of limestone, between each layer of the compost pile. Then turn the pile over.

* Use two cupfuls of wood ashes in place of each cupful of limestone to raise pH of soil more quickly.

* Wood ashes have also been used for generations as a deodorant for outhouses and chicken coops.

Don't be concerned if ashes from newspapers with black print are mixed in. The paper is made of pulpwood and the ink mostly carbon. However, don't use ashes of colored paper, such as comics or glossy magazines. Avoid ashes of wood that has been painted, especially from old houses. They may have traces of lead.

Ashes from coal or coke may contain sulfides that can be toxic to plants when wet. And some ashes may contain large amounts of iron that can be harmful to soil. If weathered for six months or more, some of the sulfides in coal and coke ashes will leach, but it's safer not to use them in the garden or on the compost pile.

Bringing in the Leaves

*Use them any way you like—
leaves are nothing but good
for your garden.*

MARK KANE

The trees in one acre of forest shed as much as two tons of leaves each fall. You may complain, as you lean wearily on a leaf rake, that your neighborhood outdoes any forest, but be thankful. Hang on to your leaves. And if your neighbors don't want them, hang on to theirs. It makes no sense to send treasure to the dump.

Fallen leaves carry 50 to 80 percent of the nutrients a tree extracts from the soil and air during the season—the carbon, potassium, phosphorus, molybdenum and dozens of other elements. Some scientists believe trees extract a little nitrogen from the air. In any case, leaves have surprising amounts of nitrogen, sometimes as much as in manure. Of the 20 elements science says are essential for plants, leaves probably have them all, *and* a few that are yet to be discovered. One test found over 50 elements in a hickory leaf nourished by mineral-rich soil. The proportions vary from one tree to the next—oak leaves have eight times the magnesium of beech leaves, for example—but your garden will be grateful for a diet of leaves of any kind.

Because their ratio of carbon to nitrogen is high (between 40 to 1 and 80 to 1), leaves are often accused, with sawdust and other woody materials, of robbing the soil of nitrogen. Whether they deserve the reputation depends partly on how they are used, as David E. Hill discovered in research conducted for the Connecticut Agricultural Experiment Station.

Hill suspected that raw leaves might be toxic to many vegetables. To test his theory, he tilled five inches of uncomposted leaves into the soil. To make sure that the vegetables had plenty of nitrogen, he fertilized and tested throughout the season. Since the leaves could not deprive the soil of nitrogen, any change in the vegetables would have to be blamed on the leaves themselves.

Of 15 common vegetables, most yielded less than the same vegetables planted at the same time on a nearby plot. The average decline was 17 percent, in spite of cauliflower and lettuce doing better with raw leaves than without them. Peppers fared worst, making half the yield of those in the leaf-free plot.

"We got the same results," Hill says, "whether we turned the leaves under in fall or left them out as mulch all winter and turned them under in the spring." Hill also says that simply mulching vegetables with raw leaves causes a loss in yields.

To check for something toxic, Hill poured water through a bin of leaves that were just starting to decompose and collected the liquid that leached out. "The tomatoes and broccoli we watered with the leachate yielded 10 to 20 percent less than the other plants." Hill's research jibes with a study in which raw organic material and immature compost both inhibited seeds and seedlings.

Before you conclude that raw leaves have no place in your garden, read the results of Hill's research: Plots that received five inches of raw leaves *outyielded* the plot that never received leaves. In fact, two

49

other plots, one amended with partially decomposed leaves and the other with leaf mold, also outyielded the control plot. Leaves in any form are better than no leaves at all.

Although raw leaves turned out to be mildly toxic to plants, the large amounts of organic matter they contributed far outweighed their ill effects. In the early tests, Hill's control plot had lots of organic matter, but without renewal, the quantity declined. Meanwhile, the plots amended with raw leaves increased in organic matter, and their yields rose. After five years of raw leaves, Hill says, the soil has been transformed: "The tilth is beautiful. The soil has improved tremendously, while the control plot has steadily declined."

The organic matter that leaves contribute to the soil is rich in cellulose and lignin. The fiber and glue of plants, they break down slowly and have long-lasting effects on the soil's tilth, aeration and moisture capacity. In tests at community gardens in New Haven, Connecticut, Hill found that the poor, sandy, rubble-ridden soil nearly tripled in moisture capacity with the addition of three inches of leaf mold. In sunny weather, plants on the leaf-mold soil took two to three days longer to wilt than plants on unamended soil. Leaf mold holds up to 500 percent its own weight in water. Good topsoil, by comparison, holds a mere 60 percent.

As leaves break down, they glue particles of soil together into crumbs—the signs of good tilth. And as the crumbs form, air spaces open in the soil, giving it the texture of leavened bread. The soil gains a greater capacity for water *and* air—it takes more rain to cause waterlogging and a longer drought to cause wilting.

If you garden on poor soil, low in organic matter, mixing raw leaves into your soil might hurt your yields the first year—slightly. But as you add leaves each season, and the amount of organic matter in your soil rises, so will your yields.

Some people say raw leaves make the soil too acidic for a garden. It's true that most leaves are acidic, with a pH below 6. (Oak leaves are often singled out, but they are not as acidic as many others.) However, as leaves break down in the soil, changes take place that raise their pH and make it less important. Even loads of leaves rarely drop the soil's pH below 6.5 or so, which is fine for most vegetables. What's more, organic matter has a buffering effect that masks the soil's acidity. With lots of organic matter, even vegetables that hate acidity will thrive.

If raw leaves don't suit your style of gardening, compost them. The books say that to be in the ideal range for composting, leaves should have a carbon-to-nitrogen ratio of 30 to 1. Evidently, when they first fall, the ratio is close enough. In Webster Groves, a suburb of St. Louis, Missouri, the city shreds its leaves and piles them 14 feet high. Within a week, microbial life is working feverishly. Plunge a hand through the surface of the pile and you feel moist heat.

Collecting free "gardener's gold"

Louis Brenner, founder of the leaf program, has measured interior temperatures in the piles of 175 degrees. "Even in winter," he says, "I've seen temperatures of 150 degrees. The weather has to get really cold—5 to 10 degrees below zero—before a slight crust of ice forms on the piles."

Unshredded leaves will compost, too. In New Haven, freshly fallen leaves are raked to the curbs, scooped up, loaded into trucks, and dumped in windrows 12 feet wide and 8 feet high. In spite of compaction from the loading (and "impurities" like grocery carts, leaf rakes and engine blocks), the windrows take only two weeks to reach temperatures of 150 to 160 degrees. Hill added ammonium sulfate, a potent chemical source of nitrogen, to one windrow with the idea that narrowing the carbon-to-nitrogen ratio would speed up the composting. To his surprise, the doped windrow did not respond. It heated up about three days earlier than the pure windrows, but both took the same time to compost. On winter visits to take the windrows' temperature, Hill found the neighborhood dogs warming themselves on the leaves.

It's clear that, whatever their carbon-to-nitrogen ratios, leaves will compost. It's also clear that they sometimes don't. Plenty of gardeners, myself included, have seen leaf piles persist for years. In his own backyard, Hill has piles that rot and piles that don't.

To get leaves to compost, pile them as soon as they've fallen. Leaves that sit for weeks unraked dry out, and moisture is as vital as air to composting. And if leaves have weathered, they'll be poor in nitrogen—it's readily washed out by rain, while the carbon is more durable. The longer a leaf weathers, the wider its carbon-to-nitrogen ratio becomes, and the less attractive it is to microbial life.

Big piles help leaves hold their heat, but piling also cuts air circulation. As microbial life uses up the oxygen in the pile, things slow down and the temperature falls to 100 degrees or so, it needs turning to recharge it with air.

For a backyard leaf pile big enough to hold heat, Hill thinks six feet by six feet is a good size, and five feet is a good height to avoid compaction. That is a lot of leaves, 180 cubic feet, or about 25 trash bags' worth. Turning a pile this size is work, and the occasional wet, heavy clumps of leaves must be teased apart. But one benefit of speedy, hot composting is the neutral pH (6.8 to 7) of the compost. Without turning, your pile will probably take several years to break down, and the leaf mold will be slightly acidic. Well-rotted leaves, despite their reputation, are not highly acid. Don't be tempted to add lime to a hot pile; you'll cause a lot of nitrogen to vaporize if you do.

Leaf compost is valuable. When Webster Groves finishes piling up its 15,000 cubic yards of shredded leaves, people line up for a share. Residents take away several thousand cubic yards for their gardens. Nurseries haul truckloads away for potting mixes, container plants and landscaping. And Shaw's Gardens, the world-famous arboretum in St. Louis, Missouri, uses the leaf compost by the ton. Three times during the season, the flower beds get a 1½-inch mulch—after the tulips flower, then after the annuals, and finally after the chrysanthemums. Each time the flowers are uprooted, the mulch is tilled in. Alan Godlewski, who supervises the plantings, says that the compost makes a difference. "In three years, the soil in the beds has risen six inches. It holds more moisture and drains better, and the mulch helped a lot during last year's drought."

Shaw's Gardens has devoted 14 acres to the re-creation of a Japanese garden, complete with a 4½-acre lake. In excavating the lake, bulldozers scraped up the heavy subsoil—unweathered gray and yellow clays—and spread it on parts of the garden site. Godlewski used tillers and disks to work three to six inches of leaf mold into the clay. The results were topsoil and thousands of visitors who admire the Japanese garden each year.

In Webster Groves, leaves are a resource. Gardeners out raking leaves are looking ahead to spring. If you follow their example, you'll see the difference leaves can make to your soil. You may find yourself wishing your neighborhood had more trees.

Weeds Build His Garden Soil

*How a Maine gardener learned
to like weeds and to use them.*

MICHAEL LAFAVORE

Occasionally, Eliot Beveridge has a weed problem. Nothing unusual about that, except that his weed problems aren't the type most of us have. What troubles Beveridge is that sometimes there aren't *enough* weeds in his garden. And when that happens, he's likely to venture out in search of weed seeds to plant in his garden. He's even been known to transplant full-grown weeds into his vegetable patch.

No, the Harvard-educated, former art teacher hasn't taken leave of his senses. Far from it. It's just that he's learned to live with weeds, maybe even to love them to some degree. Instead of looking on lamb's-quarters, redroot pigweed, purslane and burdock as garden pests, he views them as excellent soil builders, garden helpers that give back more than they take. And located, as it is, on the island of North Haven, a 16-mile strip of rocky land off the Maine coast, Beveridge's garden needs all the help it can get.

Weeds, he insists, have a lot to offer, despite their unsavory reputation. For one thing, they're good excavators, sending roots deep into the soil to bring up untapped reserves of minerals. The roots also help break up and aerate the soil and when they decay, the channels that are left help carry water into the subsoil. And, whether they're put on the compost heap or hoed directly into the soil, Beveridge contends that weeds give back to the soil much more than they have taken.

"Weeds aren't robbing and wasting the soil's nutrients, they're salvaging them," he says. "Weeds pay their own way. Like all green plants, they draw less than 5 percent of their substance from the soil. The rest comes from water and air. When they're left to decay in the soil, weeds return all your principal with 2,000 percent interest. Is that robbing?"

His benevolence extends only to annual weeds, which start anew from seeds each year. The root-running perennials he "fights to the death," because their pervasive root systems interfere with vegetable growth.

Unless an annual weed has the bad manner to sprout too close to one of Beveridge's vegetable seedlings, it is allowed to grow, at least for a while. In the spring, when a carpet of green weeds covers his garden, Beveridge looks the other way until the weeds have grown two or three inches high. Then, he hoes the tops into the soil, leaving the roots intact.

I've found that the carbon-nitrogen ratio in young weeds is just right for swift decay," he notes. "Hoeing them in at this stage gives a quick boost to the garden."

Summer weeds are usually allowed a free reign, unless they grow high enough to shade the vegetables. When the weeds are full-grown, the tops are cut off before seeding and tossed into the compost heap.

"The secret is to always keep your weeds subordinate to your crops," says Beveridge. "If they block the sun to your vegetables, cut them down with a sickle or trample them underfoot. If they aren't bothering anything, let them grow."

Beveridge says he never pulls weeds up, and when cutting the tops he makes sure the roots are left undisturbed, to rot in the soil.

"A channel left by a root that's only 1/10 of an inch thick will carry nearly a million times more water into the subsoil than disconnected pores of the same size," he says. "That's a pretty good argument for leaving the roots intact."

When fall rolls around and the vegetables are harvested, Beveridge lets his weeds grow untouched. A frugal Yankee, he wouldn't think of buying seeds for a cover crop when there is so much free weed seed available. The weedy canopy, he contends, protects his garden soil from erosion during fall rains and catches and holds drifting snow in winter.

"Snow is often called 'poor man's manure,'" he says. "It carries down nitrogen, and the blanket of snow keeps in warmth and prevents the soil from freezing as deeply."

Although he's now one of their foremost champions, it wasn't love at first sight for Beveridge and his weeds. On the contrary, he fought for years to keep his garden weed-free, running his small tiller frequently up and down the rows and pulling up any weed that dared show itself.

"I thought weeds were like nits—something nice people didn't have," he laughs.

But his overzealous cultivation, combined with the liberal use of chemical fertilizers, eventually turned his thriving garden into a hard-packed wasteland. Where once he had grown a 25-pound cabbage, nothing did well after a dozen years.

"It finally dawned on me that I was doing something wrong," he recalls. "I realized that by digging up and throwing away all those weeds I was wasting the good organic matter that my soil needed most. There was no way I was ever going to totally eliminate all the weeds, anyway. I figured if I couldn't lick them, I might as well join them."

Beveridge chucked his chemical fertilizers, gave the cultivator a rest, and began reading up on organic methods. Eventually, with the help of weed compost, seaweed and well-rotted sheep manure, he was able to restore his garden's lost fertility. At about the same time, he began collecting weed seeds and broadcasting them throughout his property to insure an adequate supply of compost material. Some of his neighbors may have begun to doubt his sanity when they saw him planting weeds when he should have been pulling them, but Beveridge's yearly bumper crops—enough to fill two large freezers and then some—made believers out of many of them. A few, he says, have admitted they're leaning towards adopting his "permissive attitude" toward weeds.

56

While the remaining doubters are out yanking weeds, Beveridge plans to spend *his* free time with an ax, rather than a hoe, in his hands, chopping the wood that helps heat the 120-year-old farmhouse where he lives with his wife, Dorothy.

"On the chopping block, I can work off the hostilities that others must expend on their weeds," he says. "It's much more productive."

An Organic Scavenger

---

*He finds treasures
to bury in his garden.*

MORT MATHER

I'm an organic bag man. But instead of shopping bags, I have a pickup truck. Because I've told everyone all around that I want "organic discards," my collecting chores are much easier. People have called me to come and pick up leaves, grass clippings, various manures, wood chips and spoiled hay.

Sometimes I feel guilty about taking such valuable items from people who could use them. I once removed a large pile of spoiled hay that was stacked right next to the owner's home garden. The winter squash patch was within a few feet of the pile of hay. I was tempted to mulch a few hills to show what the hay could do for them. Timothy hay has a conventional fertilizer value (about 1−.5−1), but beyond its nitrogen, phosphate and potassium, it will add organic matter to the soil. The organic matter will feed billions of microorganisms as they turn it into humus. These microorganisms will do more for the fertility of the soil than the minerals in the original material alone can do.

Collecting leaves in the fall may be the easiest job for the organic scavenger. I just pick a beautiful fall weekend, and while others are raking leaves, I'm cruising tree-lined streets picking up the bagged leaves left at curbside. I could refine the operation by talking to the rakers and asking when the collection truck will be by, then making sure I get there first. I usually get a load easily even without any organization. I can pick up bagged leaves at the dump on weekends if my timing is right. The trick is to get to the leaves before the dump's front-end loader covers them up.

Cemeteries, parks and motels are gold mines for leaves and grass clippings. One cemetery has been dumping all this wonderful material over a bank for many years. Then they go out and buy fertilizer, ignorant of the pile of it they have right there! Seventy-five pounds of leaves contain about as much nitrogen as a five-pound bag of blood meal, which costs around $5. The leaves are actually higher in nutrient value to the plants, which should make them worth even more money. I hesitate to say this for fear my fall ride may someday be marred by signs proclaiming, "Leaves for sale."

I once put high sideboards on my truck to haul a large load of leaves a greater distance than usual. The call had come from an amusement park 25 miles away. They also had an animal farm within the park and offered me the manure. I passed that find on to a gardener who was closer.

I don't always have to travel to find organic materials. Some are delivered. One family in our area had an immaculate horse barn. It appeared that they had found a horse that didn't produce manure. Finally I asked what they did with their horse manure. When they said they took it to the dump once a week, I pointed out that I was much closer than the dump, and that I would help unload their truck. Weekly deliveries began at once, and manna from that source continued for about a year, when they sold the horse. I mention horses and what wonderful animals they are to those people whenever I get a chance.

My wife was in a fish market watching them fillet fish one day when it occurred to her to ask what they did with the heads, tails and bones that were being thrown into a large barrel. "They go to the dump," the grocer answered. I called and arranged to pick up a barrel of scraps the next time they cut fish. You could buy fish meal at about $20 for a 50-pound bag last time I checked. Whatever the price, free fish scraps are cheaper, and you are helping your community by converting a problem at the dump into a resource in your garden. Have some nice, clean, nonaromatic compostable materials handy before you bring home the fish, as they will smell and attract flies unless put into a compost pile immediately.

One of the richest garden soils I ever saw belongs to a woman who convinced the town road crew she could use all their leaves in her garden, but only if they would dump them there. She fenced the garden but says it really isn't necessary as long as they don't dump when there is a high wind. The leaves stay on top of the soil until spring, when she turns them under.

Seaweed is a valuable fertilizer, containing a wide range of trace nutrients, as well as about as much nitrogen and more potassium than chicken manure. I know one resourceful gardener who collects seaweed far from the ocean. He belongs to a charitable organization that puts on a clambake every summer. He volunteers for the cleanup detail and takes seaweed, lobster shells and clam shells home to his compost pile.

We have an organic section in our dump because I wanted to fertilize a hayfield with seaweed. I could get seaweed at the beach in spring before the tourists arrived, but once the beaches were covered with people, the seaweed somehow disappeared.

I learned that the town crews raked it all up and took it to the dump. The dump buried its seaweed out of reach. I went to the Town Manager, who put me on the agenda for the next Selectmen's Meeting. I asked that an organic section be established at the dump, where all organic materials could be piled to be claimed by gardeners. I also suggested that the town could help by piling the seaweed they collected from the beach into this special section.

I got all I asked for and more. They fenced the area and made a special sign for it. The next time I went to the dump, there was a pile of seaweed in the fenced area. When I pulled up beside it and started forking the material into my truck, the big front-end loader that covers the landfill came lurching toward me. I thought I was going to have to explain that what I was doing was authorized. Instead, the operator asked if I wanted him to load my truck. What service!

I have come across only one organic waste I didn't like—dog

manure. I've tried to compost it, but when it came to turning the pile I found that very little composting had occurred. I don't know why the manure didn't become compost. It did rot eventually but it certainly didn't act like any other manure I have used. I have also received bags of dog hair, but I found that was also difficult to compost.

There really isn't much to becoming a scavenger of organic materials. It just boils down to seeing value where others don't. Homing pigeons are fascinating to watch, but did you know that what is to be found under their cages is 4 percent nitrogen, 2 percent phosphate and nearly 1½ percent potash? Wherever someone is working with wood, there is usually some sawdust or shavings that make an excellent addition to a compost pile too rich in nitrogen. The busier the kitchen, the more kitchen scraps it will generate. Not every professional kitchen will separate scraps for you, but if you can talk to the salad-makers in a restaurant, school or hospital, they may be willing to keep their "garbage" separate from papers, cans and glass.

Follow an animal home. Track down vegetables. Ultimately, the trail will lead to a resource that others will call waste.

Getting Sawdust to Work for You

How to turn wood waste into a garden helper.

MICHAEL LAFAVORE

You might say that sawdust, when it comes to using it in the garden, is a bit like Dr. Jekyll and Mr. Hyde. It's got a good side and it's got a bad side. Luckily, sawdust's good side is very good, and the darker aspects of its personality are easily tamed. With a little knowledge on how it behaves, you can mix up a potion that will turn this inexpensive source of organic matter into a garden ally.

First, the positive news about sawdust: It's an excellent soil-builder, capable of making heavy, clay earth loose and fluffy and increasing the moisture-holding capability of sandy soils. Sawdust also makes an excellent mulch for fruit trees, berries and many vegetables. Best of all, it's cheap—often free for the hauling.

Now the bad news: Sawdust decomposes very slowly. Unaided, it may take a year to break down. Some woods, such as pine, are quicker than others, but in general you've got to be more patient when composting wood wastes.

And while sawdust is great for increasing soil's friability, it does little to increase fertility. In short, it woefully lacks a number of important nutrients. A ton of sawdust contains only about one pound of phosphorus, two pounds of potash, three pounds of lime and two pounds of nitrogen.

Most of its nutritive shortcomings can be overlooked, but the paltry allotment of nitrogen can cause headaches, especially when you're working with fresh sawdust. The fungi and bacteria that break the material down need lots of nitrogen to do their work. Since the microorganisms can't get enough nitrogen from the sawdust, they turn to the soil for it. If a crop is growing in that same soil, the sawdust will compete for the available nitrogen and the plants will suffer.

For this reason, fresh sawdust should *never* by worked into your garden soil less than six months before planting time unless it is supplemented with a rich source of nitrogen such as blood meal, cottonseed or alfalfa meal, grass clippings, manure or compost.

By far the safest way to handle sawdust is to compost it. The easiest way to accomplish this is to simply dump a pile of the stuff in a spot you won't be needing for a while, watering and turning the material every month or so. Eventually—and it could take a year or so—the sawdust will break down to a soft, dark brown humus. If you don't want to wait that long, try adding one pound of chicken manure for every three pounds of sawdust. The manure, which is so high in nitrogen that it often burns plants when used alone, will speed up decomposition greatly, producing usable compost in about three months. And since sawdust can absorb up to five times its weight in moisture, it will prevent the manure's valuable liquid nutrients from being leached away. If poultry droppings aren't available in your area, substitute blood meal mixed with equal parts of water.

Some gardeners believe that using sawdust will raise the acidity of the soil, but there is no evidence that it does. Studies conducted at the Connecticut Station between 1941 and 1954 found no evidence that sawdust soured the soil appreciably. If your soil is already at its acidity threshold, adding large amounts of sawdust *could* tip the scales. On the other hand, if your soil is slightly alkaline, the sawdust may help neutralize it. Types of wood vary in their acidity. Some, such as cypress, are very acidic (pH 3.5 to 3.9). Others, like pine, spruce and white oak are less so (pH 4.1 to 5), and a few, including white birch, maple and red oak are only slightly acidic (pH 5.1 to 6).

It's also commonly believed that cedar and black walnut sawdust contain toxic substances that may inhibit plant growth. There's quite a lot of argument on this point. Some say composting will destroy the toxins, others contend that sawdust from these woods are unsafe. Unless you want to risk your garden, find out who's right. It's probably best to avoid cedar and black walnut sawdust.

In addition to its benefits as a soil-builder, sawdust also makes an excellent mulching material. It conserves moisture, inhibits weeds and helps keep the soil cool during hot summer months. Peach, apple and pear trees, asparagus, blueberries, strawberries and raspberries do especially well with sawdust mulches. A Canadian test found that this type of mulching increased raspberry yields by up to 50 percent.

To mulch fruit trees, first apply a layer of soybean or cottonseed meal or compost around the base. In addition to helping retain moisture, the mulch will discourage rodents, who for some reason don't like walking on it.

Sawdust makes a good all-around garden mulch as well, but its use requires some care. Because you won't be plowing it into the soil, it's safe to use fresh sawdust when mulching. But when it comes time to plow the garden under, you'll need to add a nitrogen boost beforehand in the form of manure. In the meantime, watch your plants for leaf yellowing or stunted growth, signs of nitrogen deficiency. This shouldn't occur unless your soil is not very fertile to begin with, but if it does, side-dress your plants with blood meal, compost or a dose of manure tea.

When planting small-seeded vegetables such as carrots and beets, apply a four-inch band of sawdust ¼-inch thick on top of each row to prevent the soil from crusting. For most other vegetables, wait until the plants are two inches high and put down a two-inch layer of sawdust over the area between the rows. This should keep out all but the most stubborn weeds. If some intruders do push their way through, snip them off at the base. Pulling weeds will mix sawdust into the soil, something you'll want to avoid at this point.

Finding an adequate supply of sawdust shouldn't be a problem, no matter where you live. At last estimate there were about 12 million tons being produced each year by the lumber and paper industry. Only a fraction is being used and much of the rest is burned, for lack of a better method of disposal.

If you live near a paper or saw mill, lumberyard or furniture factory, chances are good you'll be able to get all the sawdust you need for next to nothing. If there's a stable nearby that uses sawdust as bedding for the animals, ask if you can buy some. In this case, a nitrogen supplement should be unnecessary. Wood chips are fine for mulching, but shouldn't be considered as a soil amendment because of the length of time it takes for them to decompose. Also stay away from the very fine dust that is produced when wood is sanded. It will tend to pack up and exclude air from your soil, which is the opposite of what you want it to do.

If you can locate a source of ground bark, haul off as much as they'll let you have. The rich bark is more porous than sawdust and breaks down quicker. Composted with poultry manure, ground bark also makes an excellent potting mix. Studies have shown that the bark contains a substance which reduces attack from soil-borne diseases caused by fungi and nematodes. Avoid bark from trees that have been treated with insecticides.

Choosing and Using Manures

It's the basis of natural soil fertility and top production.

JAMES JANKOWIAK

Not so very long ago some livestock owners would practically pay you to haul away their accumulated manure. Not so today. Manure may not be worth its weight in gold, but its price is on the rise, and the more we learn about it, the more valuable it seems.

Manure and compost are the very best all-around fertilizers available to organic gardeners, adding humus to the soil—something *no* chemical fertilizer does. Manure releases its nutrients into the soil on both an immediate and extended basis, helping crops grow steadily throughout the season.

In fact, manure, like compost and other decayed organic matter, *is the basis of continued soil fertility.* It supplies nitrogen, phosphorus, potassium and trace elements. It furnishes carbon as a source of energy for the soil life system.

Animal manures are divided into two basic groups—hot, or those that contain a relatively high proportion of nitrogen, and cold, or those that contain a relatively low nitrogen proportion. The former includes duck, goose, hen, sheep, turkey and rabbit manure. The latter group includes cow and hog manure on the low end and horse manure on the high end. Naturally, any manure will vary in nutrient content depending on what the animal has been eating, whether or not it is pregnant, nursing or growing (in which cases the nutrients in the manure are less), and how the manure has been treated in terms of being mixed with bedding, or exposed to improper handling or leaching. However, fresh manure, with a reasonable amount of bedding or litter mixed in it (not an excessive amount), will contain the following amounts of nutrients *per ton:*

TYPE	POUNDS NITROGEN	POUNDS PHOSPHORUS	POUNDS POTASSIUM
Cow	11	3	10
Hen	22	18	10
Hog	11	6	9
Horse	13	5	10
Sheep	20	15	8

The other poultry manures will line up near hen manure. The other cold manures will line up near cow manure. In addition, there will be varying amounts of trace elements needed for proper plant growth, plus all that wonderful humus. If these amounts for N-P-K seem low, you have to remember that as commonly sold by the bag or by the truckload from farm or feedlot, manure is not straight dung, but a mixture of dung and other materials. Not only that, but manure unlocks nutrients already present in the soil, and its fertilizing value is much higher than chemical analysis shows.

For instance, poultry litter sometimes comes as a mixture of wood shavings or sawdust and droppings. Some people say that if a bedding contains a high percentage of fresh sawdust, it is not fit for the garden because it locks up nitrogen and gives off harmful acids, and encourages harmful fungus growth. I've used sawdust and shavings by the ton as poultry litter, animal bedding, and directly on the soil as an amendment or mulch, and have never noticed any harmful effects. The part about locking up nitrogen is true, but in a fertile garden this won't make any significant difference. Besides that, the nitrogen is not lost—it's released later from the decaying sawdust, which in the end is humus. So don't hesitate to use sawdust, or manure that is made with straw, especially rye straw. If your soil is heavy, manure with peat moss bedding will rot slowly and add the beneficial value of the peat to the soil. Some bedding, such as salt hay, gives a rather difficult-to-handle, close-grained product, but is otherwise fine to use. In a pinch, I've even used eelgrass. Straw tends to be a good absorber of liquid manures and has the advantage that it breaks down quickly and cleanly.

There are three basic ways manure is sold: fresh, rotted and air-dried. Fresh is cheapest, and dried most expensive. The dried costs more because the percentage of nutrients and humus is correspondingly higher. For example, hen manure that renders 20 pounds nitrogen, 16 pounds phosphorus and 10 pounds of potash to the ton will come out about 40-30-19 dried. Chicken, sheep and steer manures usually can be found dried and bagged at nurseries and even at supermarkets. But because of their cost, I recommend their use only when unprocessed manure is not easily available, or for special uses like potting, or where handling it fresh is difficult, such as for people physically unable to load and spread tons of manure.

If you do have to buy your manure instead of produce it, and you're getting it unprocessed, make sure you know something about the way it was handled or you might be getting less than you paid for. For example, if it's sold by the ton you might be buying a whole lot of water the seller sprinkled on the night before—sort of like buying wet lettuce at the supermarket. Also, you might be getting "burned" or "fire fang" manure. This is manure that has been piled up in a relatively dry state. The process of composting starts after a fashion, but then the manure heats up so hot that it actually destroys much of the nitrogen as well as ruins some of the humus value.

The other major problem is leached manure. The nitrogen, potash and phosphorus found in manure are for the most part water soluble, and that means that if the manure heap is exposed to rain, the nutrients leach out with the runoff. The resulting matter still has humus value but should not be considered a complete fertilizer.

With all these possibilities of spoiling the manure, how should we handle it? My sentiment leans in two ways. First is compost. Every time we cleaned out the hen house we had stacks of weeds, eelgrass

68

and garden trash ready near the compost bins. I started the compost heap using the chicken manure in one-inch layers over six-inch layers of green matter, and under caps of one inch of dirt. (In case you have to use other fresh manures, cow bedding should go on in two- or three-inch layers, depending on the quantity of the mixed-in straw or shavings.) The resulting compost heats up fast, turns easily and makes a rich product for general garden use.

The second use is broadcast spreading, but this presupposes that you have a lot of manure and ground to work at the same time that you have stalls or yards to clean. If you do, just haul out the manure, spread it over the ground and turn it in. Sometimes this is not the most pleasant-smelling work, but it is the best way—next to composting—to conserve all available nutrients.

If you're buying fresh manure and are not going to use it right away, or if you have a steady supply, the thing to do is to cover the day's yield or each incoming load with a layer of dirt or some organic matter like peat moss or sawdust (both of which will help absorb odors). If the manure is wet, like chicken droppings or cow dung, absorbent material like peat is best. If it is relatively dry, like horse manure, use dirt.

Keep the pile moist, but not so moist that water is running out the bottom, and not so dry that the pile can heat up uncontrolled. The last step is to turn the pile every few weeks to ensure even decomposition. The resulting material can be used at any time. However, if your object is to have rotted manure ready to apply directly to the garden, you'll have to stop adding new material at some point, and start a second heap. Allow the composting process to go its full course with the first pile and you'll have a rich, earthy smelling product after a few months that is fit for immediate application to vegetables and flower gardens.

If you haven't followed these steps and your manure is green, you must take some precautions to protect your plants if you want to apply the manure right away. Green manure, because of the active decaying process, the heat and the high percentage of available nitrogen, can harm plants if directly applied. Furthermore, some vegetables, like carrots, respond to fresh manure with undesirable altered growth, such as forming forked roots. Some experts suggest that well-rotted manure be incorporated into the soil no later than two weeks before planting. The recommendation for the fresh manure is two to three months before planting, or in the fall for an early spring crop. In all cases, the manure should be plowed under. When using fresh manure in the summer, I've turned it under a month to three weeks before planting and have had good results. When it is well mixed with a high humus content soil, the microorganisms, beetles and worms seem to get right to work so that, except for carrots and other root crops, you should discern no bad effects.

A minimum manure application is about ten tons per acre, and a generous one about 20 tons. This latter works out to about one pound per square foot of soil. To get things down to garden size, a two- or three-inch layer spread over the area to be fertilized will average out to around ten to 15 pounds per square yard. This is strictly an average because different manures have different weights. For example, cattle manure that has been packed down by animals in a feedlot operation can weigh 1,500 pounds to the cubic yard, whereas racing stable manure might just barely top 500 pounds.

If you're short on manure, don't spread it broadcast, but down the rows. I usually dig a trench about five inches deep, toss in the manure, and cover with soil. Then I make my furrows and plant. This puts the nutrients right where developing root systems will make the most use of them. Whenever I use this method, I plan on supplemental feeding later in the season. The object is not to get the manure down deep, but to mix it well into the first five or six inches of soil when you're broadcasting. If it is all in a solid layer, six inches down, it will take some time for the plant roots to get there. Meanwhile, the nutrients will be leaching downward. If evenly spread throughout the surface soil, there's a better field for root growth. A rotary-tiller is the best piece of equipment I've found for incorporating manure in this way, but a lot of elbow grease and a shovel will achieve the same results. And you can expect such an application to benefit your garden for three years—one year for the highest nutrient advantage and three years for the humus value.

There is another, less-work method than turning under your manure, and that's to simply broadcast it and let the rain take the nutrients under. If you're fertilizing an already established stand of something—say a pasture or herb bed—or just starting such a crop, you might do well to apply composted manure to the surface and hope that a well-timed rain or overhead irrigation will take the nutrients under. However, you will still lose some plant food to the air. This can be offset when you consider that the nutrients will be right at the top of the topsoil where the seedlings or the roots of shallow-rooted crops can quickly make use of them. Another plus is that topdressing doesn't disturb existing growth.

While it can be said that you can hardly apply too much manure in terms of its wonderful humus value, there is a law of diminishing returns. For example, an application of 16 tons to the acre will often produce 80 percent of what 32 tons (or double the first figure) will produce. Similarly, a manure application around woody perennials toward the end of the season could result in lush, snappy growth that could be very susceptible to winterkill. The idea is not maximum manure usage, but optimum usage as I've outlined above, or getting the best possible results without an excessive outlay of work, manure and cash.

MANURES AND THEIR USES

HORSE: Good for general fertilization. Put up in four-foot stacks, it decomposes quickly if kept moist and turned over three or four times in a six-month period. Intensive turning can speed up the process to mere weeks. Horse manure is recommended for hot-frame operating.

COW: More liquid and less strawy than horse manure. I like it for liquid manure and "tea." Bagged and dried, it's convenient to use as a seedbed or potting ingredient.

HOG: Decomposes slowly and makes a good amendment for heavy clay soils, especially when used with peat moss.

POULTRY: Good for compost making. Well-rotted, I use it to side-dress leafy green vegetables that like lots of nitrogen.

RABBIT: Use it like poultry manure or add to worm beds and use with the castings for potting mixes and seed flats.—J.J.

Where Green Manures Fit

*Timely plantings of legumes
and grains trap nutrients
and enrich garden soils.*

TONY DeCROSTA

Early autumn, just as soon as his peas are out of the ground, is when Clark Cowburn likes to plant green manure. Each year, the Ulysses, Pennsylvania, gardener follows his late peas, onions and lettuce with a winter grain cover. "As soon as I harvest a crop, I just sprinkle a few oats, rye, barley or wheat on the ground. Before the first frost hits in October, most of my garden has a nice thick, green carpet protecting it," he says. Come springtime, Cowburn's son turns the fresh stand of grain under with his tractor-drawn plow. Then Cowburn plants cauliflowers and cabbages, or tomatoes and corn— all heavy feeders that profit from the actively decaying organic matter. The vegetables thrive.

If he preferred, Cowburn could delay plowing a part of his green-manured patch during the spring, and harvest some mature grain in early July for flour or sprouts. He doesn't, though, figuring that the energy the plants put into developing their seed heads might just as well go into improving his soil. That's worth more to him he says, than the bushel or so of grain he might coax out of 1,000 square feet, one-tenth of his garden.

Laura Wicks of Lawrence, Kansas, figures differently. She finds the aroma of bread baked from homegrown grains so irresistible that she'd rather wait and harvest some grain. She gets 10 to 15 pounds from 200 square feet of garden space she keeps in fall-sown wheat. Cold weather makes the hard red winter wheat dormant, but with the first warm days of spring, the plants start to grow vigorously. By late June, the grain is ready for harvest. After cutting the wheat with an old-fashioned sickle, Laura works in the stubble, chaff and straw with a rotary tiller. Within a month, she plants either onions, beets and potatoes, or late peas, snap beans and limas.

Grains should be an integral part of any garden rotation plan or cover-cropping system. But grains don't pull atmospheric nitrogen in and build the soil. When soil-building is your purpose, select legumes according to their ability to fix nitrogen. Alfalfa and peas, plus all of the clovers and vetches, make excellent companion legumes. Common clovers (alsike, red and white) improve soil tilth and texture while bringing in 90 to 180 pounds of nitrogen per acre, second only to alfalfa, which has the ability to fix 158 to 250 pounds of nitrogen per acre.

John Acheson of Sacramento, California, grows white Dutch clover in with tomatoes. He begins this thrifty rotation by sowing the slow-growing legume in late summer, after he turns under his early bean patch. Following an early growth spurt, the clover makes little progress through the winter. But soon after the spring sun has warmed the soil, it is more than a foot high. Acheson then mows it once, using a rotary mower with the blade set low. Where he wants to plant his tomatoes, he turns under narrow strips of clover with a shovel. A week later he sets out his transplants.

Throughout the summer he keeps the tomato patch well watered. Weeds aren't a problem because the white Dutch chokes them out. Since the clover is partially shaded by the thriving tomato plants and provides its own nitrogen, it doesn't compete for nutrients. By early September, the clover is more than a foot high and gradually takes over the bed as tomato production flags. Acheson lets the clover overwinter again, and mows it down the following spring, planting tomatoes in strips adjacent to the ones he used the previous year.

Green manures are like bank vaults with a printing press inside each one: They insure that the soil's wealth doesn't get lost or stolen, while they contribute to that wealth for as long as they're in the ground.

Crop rotation with green manures is a natural way of adding fertility where it has been taken out. Alternating vegetables with any green manure crop will check soil erosion, hamper weeds, build up organic matter, and improve soil structure and tilth. The legumes also bring in free nitrogen. Some deep-rooted green manures like alfalfa supply slow-release nitrogen to crops planted after them, and also make available other elements like phosphorus, potassium and important trace minerals that are trapped in the subsoil, past the reach of most vegetables' roots. Such crop rotations have helped control a variety of pests, including cotton insects in the South, corn insects in the Midwest and sugar beet nematodes in California. They also interrupt disease cycles. There are other benefits, too. Soil scientists have found that an increase in organic matter from green manuring usually means higher concentrations of soil microbes that help liberate *even more* nutrients.

Of the three ways to supply organic matter to soils—manure, compost and green manure crops—growing green manures is the least understood by home gardeners. They have long been important in traditional farming, and in the last 100 years, researchers have been documenting the advantages. Since 1896 when researchers at the Alabama Experiment Station began experimenting with cowpeas and vetch, they learned that corn and cotton yields in a three-year rotation with legumes were four times as great as those in the same rotation without legumes. Two Ohio researchers found that sweet clover, in a two-year rotation of corn followed by oats seeded with sweet clover, produced as much corn as a field in which manure was plowed under at the rate of six tons per acre—enough to cover the soil an inch deep.

Although they do not have the concentrated richness of animal manures, green manures are hard to beat for their convenience and organic matter production. For example, a 5-pound sack of quick-growing buckwheat seed planted on a 3,200-square-foot garden can produce nearly one ton of green matter and roots in only eight weeks! To get buckwheat's benefit, all you need do is till it into your soil.

Here are some other options to help you fit green manures into your home gardening system. In some cases, they suggest ways to get more organic matter into your soil fast. In other cases, they'll help you fine-tune your soil's mineral content.

Winter Cover

If you have only enough garden space to grow the vegetables you need every year, then obviously you can't devote half that space to a legume that demands a full growing season. That's when you should choose a winter legume like sweet clover or grain like rye to plant in the fall after your vegetables are harvested. Mulching with leaves or hay over winter won't give soils nearly the same boost that green manuring does. And thick mulches will take longer to break down in the spring than green manure crops—which could delay early spring plantings. If you leave the ground bare in the fall, nutrients like nitrogen, calcium and potash will be leached out by rain. Cover crops that grow fast in cool weather quickly absorb the most easily leached nutrients and hold them safely until spring. When you till them under in spring, the nutrients are released for your vegetables.

Winter rye is the old standard green manure and cover crop to plant in the fall. In truth, winter wheat and barley can also be sown, but rye is used more frequently because it is the hardiest of all winter grains. Rye has an amazing tolerance for cold weather—seeds can germinate when the thermometer reads only 33 degrees F., and the plant can grow in the fall until the temperature drops below 40 degrees F. It resumes growth when the temperature rises to 40 degrees F. in the spring. Rye can survive a bristling 40 below zero in the dead of winter.

Rye can be established later than wheat and starts to grow earlier in the spring. It can be planted anytime from August up to mid-October in the North and even later farther south. Planting rye in late sweet corn is an excellent strategy. After frost kills the corn, the rye still has about a month or six weeks when it can grow and cover the ground.

Several legumes can also be planted in the fall. The best choices are the sweet clovers. And the best sweet clover is common white clover because it is so winter hardy. Hairy vetch is hardy, too. "Hairy vetch is our best, most stable nitrogen-fixing legume," says Wess Culwell of Fort Worth, Texas. "It comes back year after year after year." One of the side benefits of vetch is that by planting it as a fall cover, your soil will benefit from the additional 80 pounds of nitrogen per acre the legume "fixes." And that can only help next year's crops. Culwell likes to use a special cover crop mixture which includes vetch, wheat, oats, rye and Austrian winter peas. Southerners and some gardeners in the Pacific Northwest choose crimson clover as a green manure legume during the winter months. They turn it under in the spring—the way Northerners would do rye.

For Major Nutrients

If a recent soil test shows that your soil is lacking in nitrogen, phosphorus or potassium, there is a green manure that will help unlock one or all of those major elements.

For nitrogen, plant legumes. Considering its productivity, nitrogen-fixation ability, and knack for breaking up soil compaction with deep roots, alfalfa is the best choice on good, well-drained land. White clover makes an excellent second choice. In poorer soils, try soybeans, peas or hairy vetch, which do not fix as much nitrogen as other legumes, but do not demand as much of soils as alfalfa or clover.

For soils that are phosphorus-deficient, plant buckwheat. It has the reputation for growing well in hard clays, loosening them, and making them more friable. Buckwheat also has the ability to make phosphorus more available to plants that follow it. Buckwheat apparently taps into the phosphorus that is bound up in clay minerals. And it is a fast-grower, too. As green manure, it can produce three full crops in one growing season throughout much of the United States.

Legumes like clover and alfalfa have a deep taproot system with few root hairs near the surface. Grasses and grains, on the other hand, have extensive fibrous *surface* root systems which can take up potassium better. For potassium, plant a grain like wheat, rye, barley or oats because they are excellent potassium extractors.

For Minor Nutrients and Trace Elements

Tomatoes, squash or beans just won't grow? Perhaps the cause of the problem is that your soil has a zinc deficiency. If it has, plant alfalfa, which extracts and accumulates zinc efficiently. Then follow up the next year by turning the alfalfa under and planting your main crops.

In many soils, brassicas and lettuce (or alfalfa for that matter) won't thrive because the soils are molybdenum-deficient. To guarantee an adequate supply of this trace element, grow vetch, which accumulates molybdenum. You can follow that planting the next year by alfalfa or white clover, which are very efficient extractors of micro-nutrients. *Then* plant brassicas and lettuce.

Just how sophisticated you can get with your green manure plant-ing can be understood if you consider improving a soil that is low in available manganese, which is deficient in many soils. Start your rotations by planting a spring crop of alfalfa, which will accumulate manganese from the soil. Cut it as it flowers and leave the clippings in place. The next spring, follow it with a planting of oats, which need adequate manganese and which can be fed to small animals. Har-vest the grain and turn in the straw. Follow that planting with peas, which also need manganese, but which demand almost no soil nitrogen because of the nitrogen-fixing bacteria in their root nodules. You'll have readied your soil for corn or spinach, both of which are heavy feeders.

For Better Soil Texture

If you garden on clay or sandy soils, you probably know about soil aggregation. That's the way soil particles naturally clump to-gether. Clay particles, for instance, are small and tend to compact when wet. Sandy particles are relatively large and their ability to hold water is low—they dry out very quickly. Planting fibrous-rooted grains like wheat, rye, barley or oats improves soil aggregation. Their net-work of fine surface roots holds soil together just right so that water doesn't pass through too quickly or slowly. Not only do they improve the overall organic matter content of soils when they break down, but the organic matter is also thoroughly distributed between soil particles.

Fava beans can be grown during the summer in the Northern states and during the winter in the South and in parts of California. "We use fava beans as our major source of organic matter," explains John Jeavons of Ecology Action of the Mid-Peninsula in Palo Alto, California. "The beans grow anywhere from two to six feet tall, depending on the climate. If it's really hot or really cold, they only grow two feet high—but then they put down deep root systems. If it's moderate, they grow six feet high and don't put down as deep a root system."

Jeavons recommends harvesting the beans and then just incor-porating the crop residues into a compost pile instead of tilling them under in the garden. "We compost everything," he adds. "If we turned the beans under, we'd have to wait 30 days to plant our main crops. In certain wetter climates, that can be an advantage, since it discourages soil erosion. But generally, green manures tie up the ground for several weeks when you could be growing food there."

Turning Under

If cover crop top-growth is heavy, chop it before working the green manure into the soil. Use a rotary mower and cut close to help kill the crop. Make several passes to chop the vegetation into easily degradable pieces. Then use a tiller to work the plant matter into the soil. Some rotary tillers have a cutting action as well as digging and are especially effective for this job. If you've green-manured just a small area of your garden, you can spade the crop under.

The time to work in a cover crop is usually determined by the time you plan to plant a main crop in that section. Since so much of the value of cover crops depends upon their large fibrous root sys-

COVER CROP PLANTING GUIDE

CROP	N FIXED PER YEAR (AVERAGE) LBS./ACRE	SOIL PREF- ERENCE	SOIL FER- TILITY	TOLERATES LOW pH
ALFALFA	158–250	Loam	High	No
CLOVER, RED	103–151	Loam	High	No
CLOVER, WHITE LADINO	179	Sandy Loam	Medium	No
FAVA BEANS	71	Widely Adaptable	Low	Yes
BARLEY	0	Loam	Medium	No
BUCKWHEAT	0	Widely Adaptable	Low	Yes
OATS	0	Widely Adaptable	Medium	Yes
RYE, WINTER	0	Widely Adaptable	Medium	Yes
WHEAT, WINTER	0	Loam	Medium	No

tems, it's best to postpone working them in for as long as planting schedules permit. The bigger they get, the more organic matter your soil gets.

Once they're turned under, green manure crops decay quickly. To take full advantage of the renewed soil fertility, plant your main crop vegetables when the decomposition is complete—usually within two weeks after turning under. Don't plant too soon: The green manure crop needs soil nitrogen to decay. If it isn't fully rotted, your vegetables will be nitrogen-starved.

Careful timing, from sowing legumes and grains to allowing them ample time to nourish the soil, is the key to fitting green manures into your home garden plan. Anytime the ground will be bare for a month or more, consider planting one of them.

DROUGHT TOLER-ANCE	SEEDING RATE (OZ. PER 100 SQUARE FT.)	WHEN TO SOW	SOIL TEM-PERATURE FOR BEST GERMINA-TION	WHEN TO TURN UNDER
High	1/2	Spring Fall	Warm	Fall Spring
Low	1/3	Spring Fall	Cool	Fall Spring
Medium	1/3	Spring Fall	Cool	Fall Spring
Medium	8" Centers	Spring Fall	Warm	Fall Spring
High	4	Fall Spring	Warm	Spring Fall
Medium	2½	Spring Summer	Warm	Summer Fall
Low	4	Spring Fall	Cool	Summer Spring
High	3½	Fall	Warm	Spring
High	4	Fall	Warm	Spring

Digging the Right Tools

---

*Your spade may be a shovel,
when what your soil really demands
is a pickax.*

VIC SUSSMAN

Like any art or craft, gardening goes most smoothly when you work with tools that are right for the task at hand. How well do you know the tools you use? Digging the ground, for example, is basic and seems simple enough. But there are shovels with dished, pointed blades, and others with straight-edged blades. Both kinds come on short, D-grip handles or on long ones. There are similar tools (rightly called spades) with *flat*, straight-edged blades and most often with short, D-grip handles. Each of these three is suited to special digging chores.

Getting tools for breaking up compacted ground or for preparing finely textured seedbeds presents you with more choices. Well, you don't need a lot of tools or gadgets to create a prolific garden. But you do need an understanding of the special characteristics of most of them if you are to pick out tools of good quality that are appropriate to the work you'll be doing.

Many people use the words shovel and spade as though they were interchangeable and heft those tools in the same casual way. Really, each type is specialized. Shovel comes from the same root words as "shove" and "scoop." Think of shovels as earth movers. Shovels have dished blades, made for scooping up quantities of soil or other loose material. The edge of a shovel blade may be straight, but the ones for digging into the ground are slightly pointed. The blades are mounted to the handle at an angle or cant. Spade derives from root words meaning sword or blade. Spades have flat blades, designed primarily to *cut* the earth rather than lift or remove it. Spade blades are mounted to the handle with less cant, often in a straight line. Spades are best for shaping what you are digging, like cutting straight-sided trenches or carving trees to be burlapped out of the ground with perfect, round root balls.

It's possible to do the same jobs with either tool. But let's see how such simple differences affect your work as you prepare the ground for planting. First comes the business of removing the layer of sod on the potential garden. The straight edge of the spade is perfect for cutting straight borders around the sodded area. Then you can work the blade under the roots, and if it's sharp, the spade will easily cut through the roots (as a helper peels back the sod) at a uniform depth. The sod comes off in neat flat strips that you can roll up. The scooped blade and canted handle of a shovel tend to lift as you force it forward. The blade also presents a point to the roots, not a wide edge. So with a shovel you'll carve out ragged chunks of grass and roots. You can remove sod with a shovel, but it's slower and frustrating.

There is a unique tool for this job, too, a strange-looking implement called a hand sod cutter. The blade is a flat crescent fitted into a D-handled shaft. But don't buy a sod cutter for a one-time job. That's a good rule for any tool. Instead, check with local rental shops.

I can get a sod cutter for about $3 a day.

For all-purpose garden digging—cutting into the earth, lifting, turning, tossing earth—the long-handled shovel is probably best. The dished blade holds earth better as you lift earth to turn the soil or move it from one spot to another. The pointed blade enters the ground easily and the cant in the shovel handle provides lift as your foot forces the blade into the ground. A long-handled shovel gives you more leverage for digging or throwing earth, and it saves you from bending so far over as you work. Short, D-handled shovels are really for digging in cramped spaces where the longer handle would be in the way, as in deep ditches or pits.

For double-digging, spades with short D-handles are often recommended. With a shovel you can successfully make the shallow trenches that are the first step in double-digging. But the scooped blade tends to create a rounded channel instead of a squared-off trench of full depth with straight sides. A spade does a much neater job of trenching, and so you have more room to work later as you subsoil. Spades rarely come with any handle but the short kind with a D-grip. However, I have a spade with a long, shovel-type handle which makes for extremely comfortable double-digging. For cramped work, say in nursery rows digging out trees, I might prefer a short-handled spade.

Sometimes you won't be able to penetrate the ground with spade or shovel. If your soil is extremely hard-packed or stony, you first may need to break up the ground with a pickax. Picks come in various sizes, with heads weighing from four to ten pounds. Handles are usually 36 inches long. The sheer weight of the head drives the pick into the ground, and the thick handle helps you muscle big chunks loose. If you need a pickax, a four-pound head and a 26-inch handle will suffice for most garden work.

The mattock is like a pick. It's designed for those rare occasions when you're breaking ground that's clogged with thick roots. It has cutting blades on its heavy head. A mattock is also excellent for chopping up composting debris as you turn a heap. Judge a mattock as you'd judge a pick.

After you've made the trench in double-digging, you need to loosen the subsoil. Use either the spade, the pickax or the digging fork. Most often the digging (or spading) fork is recommended. Your choice of tools really should depend on the composition of your soil. Mine is a heavy clay, so I continue using my spade, breaking the sticky yellow dirt into book-shaped chunks. If your subsoil is stony or gravelly, work with a fork. The tines will slide past obstructions more easily than a spade.

Digging forks have several other very important functions around the vegetable or flower garden. After the ground has been thoroughly cultivated once, digging forks are better than shovels or spades for

82

single-digging the soil to prepare a seedbed. They're good for digging out roots in the garden or the flower bed. A whack with the back of a spading fork will break up a forkful of earth into crumbs or clean most of the earth from the root mass of dead plants or weeds.

The business ends of digging forks are all shaped about the same. The best fork for you will be heavy enough to match your strength. Most important, its steel must be well forged. You can bend a tine on a cheap digging fork if you try too much in rocky or hard-packed ground. Once bent it will bend again. Digging forks sometimes have long handles but ordinarily come with short D-handles. The advantages and disadvantages for those handles are the same as when they're on shovels.

Once you've thoroughly worked the ground, it's time to create a fine-textured seedbed. All clods must be pulverized into fine soil and large stones must be removed. The best tool for these chores is a garden rake with steel tines. Choose your rake carefully.

Rakes ordinarily come with ten to 16 tines or teeth. (There are rakes with fewer than ten tines, but they are best for children.) The more tines, the wider and heavier the tool. So size the rake according to your physique and fitness. I prefer a 16-tine, 16½-inch-wide heavy rake because I work in clay soil. I like the extra weight for breaking up clods. Other gardeners may feel more comfortable and work more efficiently with a lighter implement. Borrow or rent a few rakes before you buy one.

The length of the rake handle should be matched to your body just as you would a canoe paddle or ski pole. Stand next to an upright rake. The tip of the handle should come up to your ear or a little beyond. A rake handle much shorter will have you bending over more than necessary.

An unusual tool I like for seedbeds on my clay soil is the thatching rake. Thatching rakes have knifelike blades instead of tines. They're commonly used to pull the thatch up from lawns. But here's how I use it: after I work my soil over with a rake I'm left with lots of golf-ball-sized chunks of dirt, too small to easily chop up with the regular tines.

I switch to the thatching rake, sliding it back and forth across the bed. The narrowly spaced blades leave the topsoil looking like coffee grounds! (By the way, thatchers are designed to be slid, not lifted, so they're easy on your back.) I don't recommend a thatching rake if your soil is peppered with marble-sized stones. The blades will jam up and you'll have to stop to clear them. Nor do I think the thatcher will be much good on sandy soils which don't clod up anyway. There are several brands available, some of which are poorly made. Mine, a Cavex, is adjustable and comes with an instruction sheet. The Cavex is made by Emsco (P.O. Box A, Gurdon, Arkansas 71743).

Here are some tips on recognizing quality in garden tools. Examine the wood and metal. Handles should be smooth and straight. Rough, poorly finished wood is a sign of inferiority. It's also hard on your hands. Does the metal look smooth, or does it have a stamped-out look? Avoid metal that has either a tinny or rough look.

Most short-handled shovels, spades and forks have D-handles. Cheap tools have D-handles made of relatively thin metal formed into a loop and attached to the shaft. These handles invariably fall apart within a few seasons. Better quality D-handles are heavy-gauge steel or steel wrapped around wood, firmly fixed to the shaft. Premier quality D-grips are all wood that's shaped in special molds.

Look at the back of shovels and spades to see how the blade is fixed to the shaft. Often you'll see that the shaft has been fitted into a partially closed tube. This "open socket" fitting is not the best. Does the shaft fit firmly? If the shaft wiggles in the store, it'll soon fall apart in the garden.

Top-quality shovels and spades have closed or solid sockets. Here the blade and a seamless socket are forged from one piece of steel and the shaft is deeply fitted into the tube, creating what should be a lifetime bond. Expect to pay at least $30 for such a spade or shovel.

Forks and rakes also vary in quality. The tang and ferrule is the most common means of joining heads to shafts. The tool head ends in a rod (tang) which fits into a hole in the shaft. A metal collar (ferrule) grasps the shaft end to keep the wood tight. You hope. Shop around. The tang and ferrule arrangement is inherently weak, so you want the best workmanship you can find. Some rakes and forks are made with solid sockets. But, like most premium tools, they aren't usually found in stores.

Tools are an investment. Like your garden, they will increase in value as prices inexorably rise. But this is true only of *quality* tools. Inferior tools won't last long enough to appreciate and will have to be replaced. Well-made tools not only endure, but they feel good in use, enhancing our work. When it comes to buying tools, follow an old adage: buy the best you can afford.

Most manufacturers actually have two or three lines of tools. They make both cheap or mediocre tools for the mass market and quality tools for the professional. In hardware stores you usually see cheap and mid-range tools. Buy the mid-range at the least. Ask to see the store catalogs listing the top-quality tools that must be specially ordered. Premium tools may also be purchased by mail. So just don't grab any old tool off the rack until you're *sure* you can't do better. In Europe, many people traditionally pass their tools on to the next generation, which says something good about both their tools and their values.

How to Translate Your Soil Test Into Soil Treatment

M. C. GOLDMAN

When I started to garden, I went along for several years adding what I *thought* my soil needed for good results. The returns I reaped in vegetables and fruits, especially tomatoes, were fairly satisfactory. Not until I took a soil test, though, did I discover that one of the main plant foods—in my case potash—was in short supply. Once I began making up that deficiency, plus continuing a program of organic fertilizing, my results and enjoyment have sprinted ahead like racing greyhounds after a mechanical rabbit.

Soil testing is one very practical way to learn more about the make-up of any soil. The two big steps to making the most of this idea are:

1.) TEST YOUR SOIL. Dig into it and find out what's there—and what isn't. By any one of several available testing methods (which are discussed a little further on), get a dependable analysis of the essential plant nutrients your soil contains—how much or how little of each. Check, too, on its acid-alkaline status (pH) to be sure this condition is favorable for the crops you want to grow. And, if at all possible, determine the percentage of organic matter it now holds, since this factor is also a mighty important one in any soil. Make the tests periodically, often enough to stay aware of changes and how well your treatment is working. After all, a good mechanic won't start repairing a car without checking it over thoroughly, nor would a good doctor prescribe for a patient without an examination.

2.) TREAT YOUR SOIL. Treat it according to the test results. Decide on a program of fertilizing that matches up supply with demands shown in your soil's check-up. Keep in mind the particular or heavy drain of any elements by specific crops you may grow. Add whatever is needed to overcome any extreme of acidity or alkalinity. Work to increase the soil's organic matter content, which is literally its "life-line" and exerts the greatest influence on desirable tilth, good drainage and moisture-holding capacities, response to other fertilizers, and all-round richness. Treat your soil right—with natural materials. Plan and prepare to use organic sources of the nutrients your soil and plants need, along with natural ground rock supplies of the minerals. Make your treatment program one that builds the soil and lasting fertility—not an artificial stop-gap measure that temporarily treats symptoms rather than causes of deficiencies in the land.

Types of Tests Available

There are two basic ways to test soil accessible to the average gardener or farmer. First and simplest of them is the home soil-test kit, which is marketed commercially and has been used successfully by many thousands. The kit provides solutions and guides for determining the approximate content of the 3 major soil nutrients—nitrogen (N), phosphorus (P) and potash (K)—plus a similar means of establishing the pH standing. Home testing kits are easy to use, require no knowledge of chemistry or laboratory procedure. One of their biggest advantages is that they permit you to make frequent on-the-spot tests of your soil (whereas other methods are often delayed) and help you adapt a fertilizing program in accord with your soil's prime needs.

The test is made simply by putting a small portion of the soil sample in a test tube and then introducing one or two "reagents." A reagent is a chemical which reacts with the nutrient being tested, and shows the quantity of the nutrient available by changing color. Color charts are supplied with the kits, and the final analysis is made by checking the color of the solution in the tube with the test chart for the nutrient being tested. Although they do not analyze for closely detailed percentages, home soil test kits used with moderate care do give the gardener a good estimate of the state of his soil—and are a valuable tool in better gardening and soil care.

The other general way to have soil tested is to send a sample to a laboratory offering this service or to your state experiment station. Farmers, rural homesteaders and city gardeners frequently get help and information through their county agent. Most state experiment stations charge a small fee for the soil test report, which in addition to an NPK and pH analysis may include indications of trace element levels and organic matter content.

A test for nitrogen, incidentally, can be used as a rough guide to the humus or organic matter condition of the soil, as there is a very close relationship between nitrogen content and humus content. High nitrogen generally means a high humus rating.

Taking a Soil Sample

Whether it is for your own home-kit test or for use by the extension station or an independent laboratory, the soil sample you take is all-important. What any test shows obviously depends on the sample, and so this small part that is to represent your soil in the examination must be taken carefully. Briefly, here are the steps in taking a soil sample:

Assemble your tools, making sure they and the containers to hold samples are clean and free of foreign matter. Be especially sure there are no residues or fragments of fertilizer, which can throw the test results completely off. Your digging or sampling tool may be a spade, trowel, garden dibble, narrow shovel with straight sides, or a soil auger or probe. For gathering samples, use a large bucket or similar container; coffee cans or small cardboard boxes which will hold about a pint of soil will serve for the final samples.

Soil samples can be taken at any time during the year that weather conditions permit. The soil should be free of frost and fairly dry. If the garden area is quite large, taking a composite, or mixed, sample from several points will provide more information than a spot sample. (Note, however, that a combined sample from two distinctly different soil types would not be a suitable representative of either one. In a case like this, individual samples would be better.)

For a composite sample, start at one end of the plot and with the garden tool cut straight down about 6 to 8 inches and lift out a narrow slice; lay this to one side. Then take another thin slice, about ½ inch, from the same section and put it in the bucket or collecting container. Shovel the first slice back in place. Now move about 6 feet in any direction and repeat the operation. Continue until the plot is given an over-all sampling. On a field of an acre or more, samples can be taken several rods apart.

Once you've covered the area to be tested, mix the samples thoroughly in the bucket and remove one pint of soil. Spread this "homogenized" sample where it can continue drying, and when completely dry and without lumps place it in the sample container. Damp or wet soil will give false test readings. Next, label the soil sample, indicating where and when it was taken, the type of crop grown last season and the type of crop to be planted this year.

Remember, soil tests can be no better than the samples tested. To reflect an accurate picture, they should be as representative of the area as possible; otherwise the story told by the test will not be true. A pint of soil—is about 1/150,000,000 part of an acre. A level teaspoonful—the amount actually tested—is 1/1000 part of a pint.

What Test Results Mean

No matter which way you get your soil tested, the results can be of value only if you understand and use them. NPK readings secured with a home soil-testing kit are generally expressed as "high," "medium" and "low" or as "abundant," "adequate" and "deficient" for each major nutrient. Acid-alkaline tests range from neutral to slightly or highly acid, or slightly to very alkaline. Laboratory and extension tests usually report percentages of the major elements and a pH reading expressed in acidity-alkalinity scale figures. (7.0 is neutral; readings below that are progressively acid; above, increasingly alkaline.)

Some test kits and most station or laboratory reports also make recommendations for improving weak or very deficient nutrient levels shown in the test. The important point for gardeners who want their soil enriched in a way that does the most good is that they translate any general or chemical recommendations into natural fertilizers—organic materials that deliver long-lasting benefits and improve the soil's composition.

Supplying Enough Nitrogen

Let's look at the major nutrients and consider how each one can be supplied when a soil test shows a deficiency. Nitrogen, of course, is one of the most vital elements for a productive soil, and one which must be constantly renewed. It is directly responsible for the vegetative growth of plants above ground. With a good supply, the plant grows sturdily, matures rapidly, and has good foliage color, food value and flavor. On the other hand, excess nitrogen—such as is forced into the plant by chemical "shot-in-the-arm" fertilizers—causes weak, watery growth, lowered disease and pest resistance, and poorer color, taste and nutritional value. Moreover, synthetic nitrogen supplies are quickly leached or washed out of soils, and the plants soon become starved for this essential element.

If your test shows a low nitrogen level, start applying one or more of the rich natural sources.

Filling in Phosphorus

Phosphorus plays a leading role in plant nutrition. It's essential for healthy growth, strong roots, fruit development and resistance to diseases. Phosphate deficiency is considered by many agronomists to be the prime factor in limiting crop production.

When a soil test points to phosphorus shortage, get busy adding a healthy natural supply. Best source is rock phosphate, ground to a meal or powder, which contains about 30 percent phosphoric acid. Colloidal phosphate, also a natural mineral product, is found chiefly in Florida in sedimentary deposits of soft phosphate with colloidal clay. It contains from 18 to 25 percent phosphoric acid.

Pulling Up Potash

Potash is the mineral that concerns itself mainly with plant's carbohydrate manufacture. As one of the "big 3" soil nutrients, it is essential for the development of strong plants, particularly in overcoming disease susceptibility and maintaining balanced nitrogen use. Plants lacking potash do not resist heat or cold well, and their process of photosynthesis is slowed down.

If a potassium deficiency shows up in your soil test, look to one of the naturally occurring materials rich in potash to bolster it. Granite dust or granite stone meal—often called ground rock potash—is a highly recommended source. Its potash content varies from 3 to

5½ percent, sometimes more. Modern machinery can pulverize rock materials to such fineness that nutrients become available for plant assimilation in relatively short periods of time, depending on the condition of the soil to be treated. Potash rock helps supply both a short-term and long-range release of its mineral content and is one of the most effective potassium fertilizers.

Greensand or greensand marl, an undersea mineral deposit, is an excellent potassium supplier (7 percent) and also contains beneficial quantities of many trace elements, some lime and phosphorus. Plant residues, manures and compost also bring potash to the soil in a free and available form. This is important because even in fertile soils the supply of free potassium is seldom enough to meet the needs of a growing crop.

Steadying the pH

The acid-alkaline (pH) balance of your soil is important because a lopsided pH will block the release of major and minor plant foods. A soil that is too acid will not release "unavailable" nutrients properly; neither will a soil that is too alkaline. Most vegetables, field crops, fruits and flowers do best on soil that is slightly acid to neutral—a pH reading of about 6.5 to 7.0. A few plants, like camellias and azaleas, need a quite acid soil; some, such as the clematis, thrive on alkaline soils.

If a test indicates your soil is too acid, use natural ground limestone or materials like wood ashes, bone meal, dolomite, crushed marble and oyster shells, all of which contain liberal amounts of lime.

For alkaline soils, materials such as cottonseed meal and acid peat moss are very effective. Leaf mold, sawdust, wood chips and other acid mulching materials will also help. Actually, organic matter is the best way to remedy either a highly acid or alkaline soil because it tends to neutralize both excesses, and acts as a buffer against adverse pH levels while it is doing this.

Keep in mind, of course, that a soil test is not the only reliable check on the soil's needs and the requirements of the plants growing in it. A soil test reveals the *available, soluble* nutrients, and these constitute about 3 percent of the total minerals present in the soil.

An accurate soil test can help prevent deficiencies, and thereby serve as a valuable tool for the average gardener.

Humus Test Helpful

A test for the humus content of your soil, by the way, is a good idea because it will show how successful you've been in adding vital organic matter. Soils in the U.S. today average 1.5 percent humus, but our country's virgin soil contained 4 percent. In a survey we conducted a few years ago, we found the average organic gardener has about 2.5 percent organic matter. You can see there's room and need for improvement.

The more you know about your soil, the better you can use it. Soil tests and intelligent treatment as a follow-up to what they show can do a lot for your gardening success

---

THE NUMBERS GAME

What does it mean when your test indicates that your garden needs 50 pounds of 5-10-10? The first number indicates the fertilizer contains 5 percent nitrogen (N), the second is 10 percent phosphorus (P), and the third is 10 percent potassium (K). Fifty pounds of 5-10-10 translates to 2½ pounds N (5 percent of 50, or .05 × 50), 5 pounds of P (10 percent of 50, or .1 × 50) and 5 pounds of K (10 percent of 50, or .1 × 50).

What about organic fertilizers? Horse manure is rated at .44-.17-.35. So to find the amount of horse manure needed to give you 2.5 pounds of nitrogen, divide 2.5 by .44 percent (2.5 ÷ .0044 = 568). The 568 pounds of horse manure will also give a little less than one pound of phosphate (568 × .0017) and two pounds of potassium (568 × .0035). You still need 4 pounds of phosphate and 3 pounds of potassium.

Let's get our potassium with wood ashes which are rated at 0-1.5-7. Three pounds divided by .07 is 43 pounds of wood ashes. You get an added bonus of about half a pound of phosphate.

Now you only need 3½ pounds of phosphorus. Rock phosphate might be rated at 0-20-0 with 4 percent available. The available figure means that 4 percent of the rock phosphate is water soluble. So if you need phosphorus that's immediately available, you should use 0-4-0 as your guide. Three-and-a-half pounds divided by .04 yields 87 pounds of rock phosphate to round out the fertilizer requirement.

As the soil test is merely a guide, so are the figures arrived at through these calculations. The ratings for various organic materials found in nature will vary from season to season, and climate to climate. Of course, the handling, age and water content will also make a difference.